OFFICIAL

Contents

So You Want To Buy A Used Car 4
Driving a used car once carried with it a social stigma. But times have changed. Here are the pros and cons of used car buying and how this book can help you buy a good used car.

Where To Find Used Cars 7
Where you buy your used car can be as important as the car itself. Here are the nine most common sources of used cars with the advantages and disadvantages of each.

How To Shop For A Used Car 16
Being an aware consumer is more than half the battle in buying a good used car. Read this chapter and raise your awareness.

Checking Out A Used Car 23
A used car that looks good is not necessarily a good used car. You must check out the mechanical condition to be sure. Here's how to do it.

Wheeling And Dealing 43
We can't make you into a wheeler dealer overnight. But we can help you get the best possible deal on your new used car.

Financing Your Used Car 50
Once you've found the car, the next step is paying for it. Shopping for financing can be just as tricky as shopping for the car itself—unless you know how.

Selling Your Present Car 57
Your present car is an important part of dealing for a new used car. So make it count by getting top dollar for it. Here the tables are slightly reversed. You're the salesman.

Do-It-Yourself Repairs And Maintenance 63
If you're dollar conscious—and buying a used car is certainly reflective of that—then you should consider do-it-yourself repairs and maintenance.

COVER: Photography by Marvin Nudelman.
Special thanks to Briggs Chevrolet in South Amboy, New Jersey and Shore Motors in Manasquan, New Jersey for the generous use of their facilities.

So You Want To Buy A Used Ca

Remember when driving a used car carried with it a social stigma of the lowest sort? Kind of like the guy who didn't love baseball, hot dogs and apple pie.

Today, it's a vastly different story thanks to current economic conditions. The auto remains a basic necessity in our highly mobile society. But inflated costs for raw materials and labor, coupled with the additional expense of meeting government anti-pollution and safety requirements have skyrocketed the price of new cars beyond the reach of many Americans. The used car has become more than a practical proposition. To many, it's a necessary proposition. No wonder that used cars outsell new cars by three to two.

Everybody drives a used car

There is no stereotype used car because any automobile outside a new car showroom is a used car. Drive a brand new car around the block and it is considered used by a prospective buyer.

In addition, no two used cars are exactly alike. Differences in mileage, driving habits of previous owners, maintenance—or lack of same—all have a bearing on the desirability, value and practical number of miles remaining in an automobile.

The average car is made to last about 100,000 miles. Life really would be simple if we could just look at a car's odometer and deduct the mileage from 100,000 to determine how much life a car has left. Such is not the case, however. Abuse, neglect and accidents can prematurely age a car to a point where the cost of necessary repairs can exceed the car's value. The shrewd buyer will notice the telltale signs that indicate a car's true condition. This isn't always easy. Sellers can be very shrewd and many have developed tricks to conceal a car's shortcomings.

New vs. used

There are both advantages and disadvantages to buying either a new or used car. Both can provide years of comfortable, reliable transportation. A new car has the advantage in buyer protection. You don't have to concern yourself about the condition of a new car because all of its components and systems are new. And while some used cars may come with a warranty, these can't compare in scope and duration to the new car warranty.

This is the rule. But you're probably familiar with the exception—the lemon. Occasionally, a new car will cause its owner grief that even repeated trips to the dealership don't seem to alleviate. Eventually, a point is reached where the warranty expires and the owner has to start paying for repairs out of his own pocket. But even so, the time and aggravation of repeated service trips can make even the benefits of the warranty seem insignificant.

There is nothing quite like the satisfaction of driving the latest and greatest. If status is your bag, nothing will fill the bill like a new car. Ride, comfort, handling and performance—they're all at their peak in the new car.

The trend in new cars is for less frequent service intervals. Spark plugs on some models are designed to last over 20,000 miles and oil changes, 6000 miles. Special high-energy ignition systems offer improved reliability and, along with other modifications, are helping to improve fuel economy over previous models.

The disadvantages in owning a new car can be summed up in one word—cost. The biggest expense in owning a new car is depreciation, or the market value that the car loses from year to year. On the average, a car loses about 30% of its value the first year. The rate of depreciation tapers off after the first year and will vary according to car, age and market conditions. Since the value of a new car is relatively high, finance charges when the car is purchased and the cost of collision and comprehensive fire and theft insurance will also be high.

Certain maintenance items may also be more expensive. You might be able to live with a small fender ding on a used car. But on your brand new baby, it stands out like the proverbial sore thumb.

Another disadvantage of new cars is their complexity due to all the now required safety and emission control equipment. Some service facilities are not equipped to handle some of the new systems and the car may require special expensive equipment for proper service. One mechanic, looking under the hood of a new car was quoted as saying, "There's so much spaghetti under there, I don't know whether to fix it or eat it."

Used cars enjoy some unique advantages. After the 1968 model year, federal anti-pollution and safety regulations forced manufacturers to build cars that suffered from some driveability problems, poor fuel mileage and downright inconvenience—like the seat belt interlock system in model year 1974. The regulations grew more strict with each passing year and some of the problems got worse, especially after the 1971 model year. The older cars didn't have such burdens and offered relatively livelier performance and better fuel economy. High compression engines, while requiring premium grade fuel, are

Your friends won't think less of you if they find you shopping for a used car.

more efficient than the later engines designed to run on regular grade no-lead fuel. Not having some of the weight-adding safety devices, these older cars were cheaper to build and more economical to operate. Of course, the older the car, the greater the chance that the car will be in poor condition. So this is a two-edged sword.

A used car gives your dollar more flexibility. If you have x dollars to spend for a car, you are more or less limited in your selection of a new car. Not so when you shop used. For the price of a new compact you can buy a luxury car that's two or three years old and still in prime condition. Remember, the smallest compact can deliver the same total number of miles in its lifetime as a big luxury car.

Your used car dollar will also buy you a greater selection of options and accessories than comparable new car dollars. An automatic transmission, for example, will cost over $200 extra on a new model. It might not affect the basic price at all on a used car.

Unlike the beating you take with new car depreciation, you can actually make used car depreciation work for you. Cars depreciate at different rates depending on popularity, market factors, etc. Some show a marked drop in value during the first two or three years, while others hold their value during the same period. If you prefer to drive a relatively late model car every year, but can't afford a new one, choose a car that depreciates very little during the second and third years. Buy when the car is one year old and trade it the next year. You'll lose very little in depreciation.

If economical transportation is more important to you, choose a car that depreciates rapidly during its second and third year, but levels off after that. Buy the car when it's three years old. Since most of the depreciation has already taken place, the price will be reasonable. Keep the car three or four years. At the end of this period, the car's value (depreciation-wise) will not be substantially less than when you bought it.

The main disadvantage to buying a used car is that it's an unknown quantity. What's in store for you? A big repair bill, or economical and reliable transportation? A thorough inspection takes some of the guesswork out of buying a used car but doesn't completely eliminate problems that can crop up down the road. The minimal or nonexistent guarantees that characterize used car sales agreements are not confidence inspiring either.

About this guide

That's where we come in.

This book is designed to help you become a shrewd used car buyer. It tells you how to shop, where to shop and what to shop. It guides you every step of the way in the sometimes frightening world where cars are in limbo between owners. It reveals the tricks of the used car trade and shows you how to see beyond the surface gloss of a car to size up its true mechanical worth.

Selecting a sound used car is only half the story. In the following chapters, you'll learn how to purchase that car at the lowest possible price. We'll tell you how to bargain toe to toe with the used car salesman to get the best deal. We'll tell you how to get top dollar for your car whether you trade it in on another car or sell it privately for cash. And if you are selling your present car, we'll pass along some tips on putting together an effective ad. We'll also show you how to read between the lines of the used car ads so you won't waste your time chasing all over town for a car that's not suitable for your needs.

Other chapters of the Official Used Car Buyers Guide will save you many dollars by revealing the pitfalls involved in financing and how to get the best deal on auto insurance. Lastly, we'll tell you how to maintain your new used car so it will provide reliable transportation and bring top dollar when it's trade-in time.

Make the maximum use of the charts and tables in this guide. When inspecting the condition of a used car, for example, go down the items in the checklist one by one. That way you can be sure of a thorough evaluation.

Now turn the page and get ready to learn all there is about used cars.

Quick Facts: Buying New Vs. Used

	Advantages	**Disadvantages**
• New Cars	Strong warranty More reliable More status Optimum ride, performance and comfort Less maintenance	High initial price High initial depreciation High cost of insurance (collision & comprehensive) Harder to service
• Used Cars	Low initial price More selection within price range Many options at no extra cost Less depreciation Less expensive insurance	Unknown quantity Minimal or no guarantees

Where To Find Used Cars

New car dealers are a good source for clean used cars because they take trade-ins on new cars.

Unlike new cars which are sold only through franchised dealers, used cars are available through many sources. These can range from your Uncle Farley or a co-worker to your local service station, to an independent used car dealer to a government auction. Each source has its intrinsic advantages as well as risks.

New car dealers

The franchised new car dealer is automatically in the used car business because he takes trade-ins on new cars. These trade-ins are either sold to the public or wholesaled to other used car dealers. As a general rule, new car dealers will keep the best of their trade-ins on their own lot and wholesale the less desirable cars. By so doing, they avoid the time and expense needed to put a poor car back in shape and they can maintain a good selection of late model cars.

The reputable new car dealer, in effect, takes some—not all—of the guesswork out of used car shopping because he has most likely screened out the clunkers from his lot.

Comparatively high overhead costs mean he has a great deal to lose by developing a bad reputation. You are a used car customer now. But next time around, you may be out for a new model.

A new car dealer's high overhead costs mean that his used cars will not be the lowest priced. Most dealers add a percentage to the car's wholesale price to cover overhead and profit. The higher the overhead, the higher the price.

The new car dealer generally offers some sort of guarantee with the car, and his expected expenses on this also have been figured into the price. Some new car dealers may be reluctant to take your car as a trade on another used car. Remember, their primary business is new car sales. Trade-ins are merely an accommodation. If the offer they make on your present car is ridiculously low, their motive is to have you try to sell it privately.

While new car dealers generally are above-board businessmen, there always are the exceptions. If you don't know a dealer's reputation first hand or by word of mouth, check him out through the local

Better Business Bureau, Chamber of Commerce or consumer organization. A good dealer has a good reputation in the community.

One thing to look out for are "bird dogs"—people who point you to a specific dealer and get a kickback on any subsequent sale. These may be people with whom the dealer does business, such as gas station operators, lawyers or bankers. One tipoff to a dealer's integrity is the way he advertises. Slick phrases like "guaranteed lowest prices," or "giving them away," should raise some doubts about doing business with that dealer.

Look for a dealer who is more conservative and candid in his advertising.

The glitter lots

The cream of the franchised new car dealers are called glitter lots. They are located in the high rent district of town and cater to the area's well heeled car buyers. These customers generally trade in their new cars every 12 to 18 months, and the mileage on these cars seldom exceeds 25,000. On some glitter lots, the rule is half that many miles. These cars generally are loaded with options and accessories and have been meticulously maintained—often by the dealer. When this is the case, the cars are called "house" cars, the dealer knowing the car's entire service history. These are the most desirable used cars on the market.

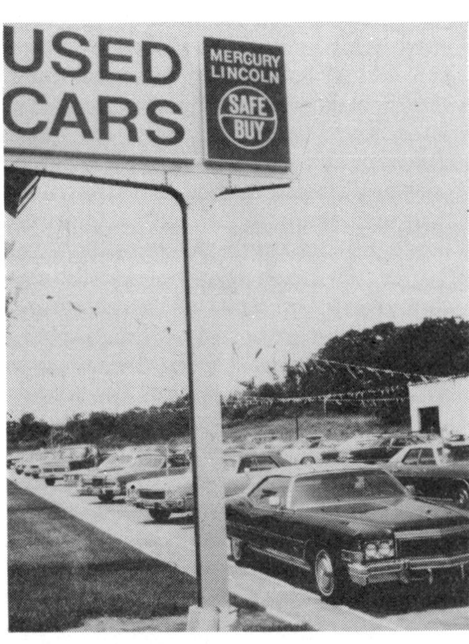

Glitter lots are located in wealthy parts of town and offer the best in used cars.

The high roller owners not only have the dealer's service department track down every squeak and rattle, they may contract for regular monthly service where the cars are brought into the shop and checked from bumper to bumper whether they need it or not. Used car prices on these lots may not be as high as you think.

Since the dealer's clientele trades in their cars at regular intervals, it's not uncommon for other customers to reserve a particular car in advance. Mr. Jones, for example, may have a standing order with the dealer for Dr. Smith's Cadillac when it's traded in every year.

These lots generally carry only the super cream of the used car crop. They wholesale trade-ins to other dealers that don't measure up to their high standards.

The main problem with glitter lots is finding them. They don't usually advertise or indulge in promotional hoopla. You can seek them out by driving through the wealthiest parts of town. If you don't happen to live in the same area as the glitter lot, it may be inconvenient to obtain dealer service should this become necessary.

The independent used car dealer

The independent dealer handles used cars exclusively. He obtains his merchandise by buying wholesale from new car dealers (remember, the new car dealer keeps the best goods for himself), from auctions and by accepting trade-ins. Consequently, his cars are not as select as those reposing on the new car dealer's lot. But his prices usually aren't as high either. The independent has lower overhead costs than the new car dealer and calculates his prices by adding a markup to the price he paid for the car.

The same cautions apply in selecting an independent dealer as a new car dealer.

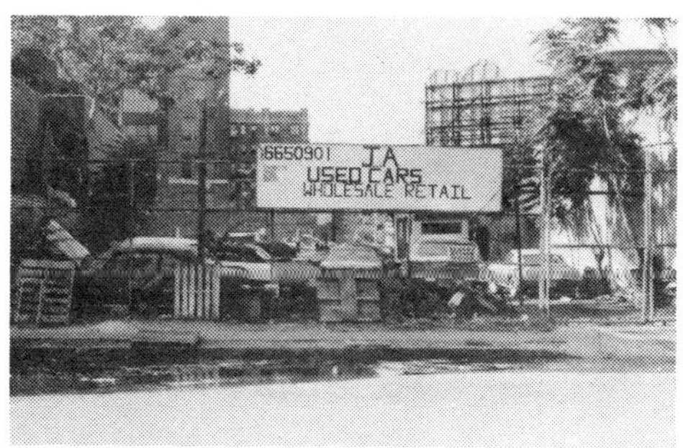

Independent used car lots come in all shapes and sizes. Car quality also varies.

Some independents rely on repeat business and have established a good reputation in the community. They will sell cars that are mechanically sound and stand behind them with some sort of warranty.

Others will skillfully cover up a car's poor health and serve it up to an unsuspecting customer. These latter dealers have done for the used car business what the Boston Strangler did for door-to-door salesmen. Government regulation and competition from new car dealers have prompted many of these dealers to clean up their act or go out of business. But the fact remains that they will handle cars that no one else will touch, like used fleet vehicles, police cars and taxis that have accumulated enough high and hard mileage to make them practically worthless. Some of these shady operators are found in the poorer sections of town where they cater to buyers who are bad credit risks. Ads claiming "no money down" (rarely true) or "guaranteed credit" pull in the customers. The down payment on these low-buck specials usually covers the dealer's cost on the car and the payments are pure profit. If the buyer defaults, the car is repossessed and sold again, increasing the yield on the dealer's original investment.

On the other hand, these dealers provide a source of automobiles to certain segments of the population that otherwise would find it impossible to obtain an automobile because of lack of money or credit. Since he takes more risks, this dealer is more prone to being ripped off by the customer who defaults on payments and skips town with the car.

If an independent dealer offers a guarantee with his car, look over his service facility. If it is sloppy or poorly equipped, it's not realistic to expect top notch service. The office and sales areas also indicate the calibre of the operation. In many cases a clean looking establishment is a reflection of a well run business.

Consignment sellers

These people do not own the cars they sell. An agreement is worked out between the owner and the consignment seller in which the owner sets the minimum price he wants. Anything the seller can get above that price is considered commission. Or the owner may pay the seller a flat fee. Gas stations, repair shops or even a neighborhood shade tree mechanic who has developed a successful sales technique are examples of consignment sellers.

A neighborhood service station may sell cars on consignment for an arranged fee.

Auto auctions may be a fun way of buying a used car, but bargains are rare finds.

Owners will consign cars for sale to save themselves the time and hassle of negotiating with a series of prospective buyers. A consignment seller may have several cars on hand at one time, offering the used car shopper a selection.

A word of caution about consignment sellers. When an owner discovers that his car has developed the beginning of a serious malfunction, say an automatic transmission problem, he may decide that it's not worthwhile repairing. Since the problem is likely to be spotted by an experienced used car dealer, the owner has his local service station temporarily mask the problem and sell the car. Of course, not all consigned cars are candidates for the boneyard. But it pays to be extra careful. The consignment seller is not licensed as are used car dealers, and you won't receive a guarantee. You have no recourse against the seller even if the engine falls out two blocks away from where you purchased the car.

Auto auctions

Dealers buy their cars at auctions. So why can't you? Most auto auctions are restricted to dealers. But there are those that allow you to attend and bid on cars.

Dealer or commercial auctions are just a new sales wrinkle. Buyers often bid up the price of cars to the point where they could have bought them for the same price from a dealer. The auctioneer will often have shills in the audience to make sure the bidding reaches a minimum level. It may be more fun to buy a car this way and you think you're getting a bargain. But you're not. Chances are, your selection may be limited, because there isn't sufficient time for the auctioneer to put his entire stock on the block. Depending on the particular auction, your opportunity for pre-sale inspection also may be limited to some degree and you may not be able to road test the car either. Auctions are time consuming. So unless you're not pressured for a car or you consider auctions a form of entertainment, stay away.

Repossession or liquidation auctions

These auctions should not be confused with dealers advertising repossessed cars. They are conducted by banks offering cars they have repossessed because the owner defaulted on his payments. From a selfish point of view, it's a way of profiting by someone else's misfortune.

Similar to these auctions are the court ordered liquidation auctions. In this case, a commercial business goes bankrupt and the court orders the firm's assets auctioned off to pay the creditors. If the company owns cars or trucks, these also are put on the block.

Likewise, if a person has outstanding debts after he passes on, some of his possessions, including automobiles, will be ordered by the courts to be sold under the gavel. This is called an *estate auction*.

You'll find the same limitations concerning selection, inspection and road tests. You'll also find dealers and other bargain-minded buyers bidding against you. So while you might obtain a good car at a good price, don't expect to walk away with any spectacular values.

Repossessed autos may not have been properly maintained by their former owners.

Government auctions

All levels of government from the federal down to the municipal regularly dispose of their motor vehicles through public auctions. While government agencies usually have periodic maintenance programs, most of the vehicles are subjected to hard use and may have excessive mileage. Decommissioned police cars are a prime example. The government usually is more straightforward than used car salesmen in describing their wares. But you may not get the chance to see, let alone bid on the really good stuff because select local dealers sometimes have an arrangement to automatically take fleet cars as they become available. Here again, you'll be rubbing elbows with dealers, some of whom will buy the clapped out machinery, and after disguising its history, place it on their lot as the special of the week.

You can find out about federal auctions by contacting the General Services Administration's Business Service Center in the nearest major city.

Rental and lease cars

Car rental and leasing companies change their fleet once a year, or whenever a vehicle has accumulated a predetermined number of miles. These cars may be sold at auction and many find their way to dealers' lots as a late model, budget priced special. Some buyers at a public auction may not even be aware that they're bidding on a rental car. While most lease and rental cars are wholesaled to the trade, one of the largest car rental firms has a policy of selling their cars directly to the public. They even have showrooms to display their most attractive wares.

A word of caution here. Stay away from the rental cars. Most have been put through the mill by a great number of drivers, many of whom feel that their rental dollar entitles them to inflict maximum abuse on the machinery. The lease car is a different story. It is usually driven by one person over a period of time and it's more apt to be better treated and maintained. There are exceptions, however. Most rental and lease cars are sold as they stand. But some of the larger agencies have limited guarantees and even financing available.

A parting word about auctions. While it is possible to obtain a sound car at lower prices than you would pay on a dealer's lot, remember, there are no guarantees with the cars, financing usually is not available and you won't be able to trade in your present car.

Buying privately

About half of all used car transactions occur between private individuals. If you know who you're buying from, be it a

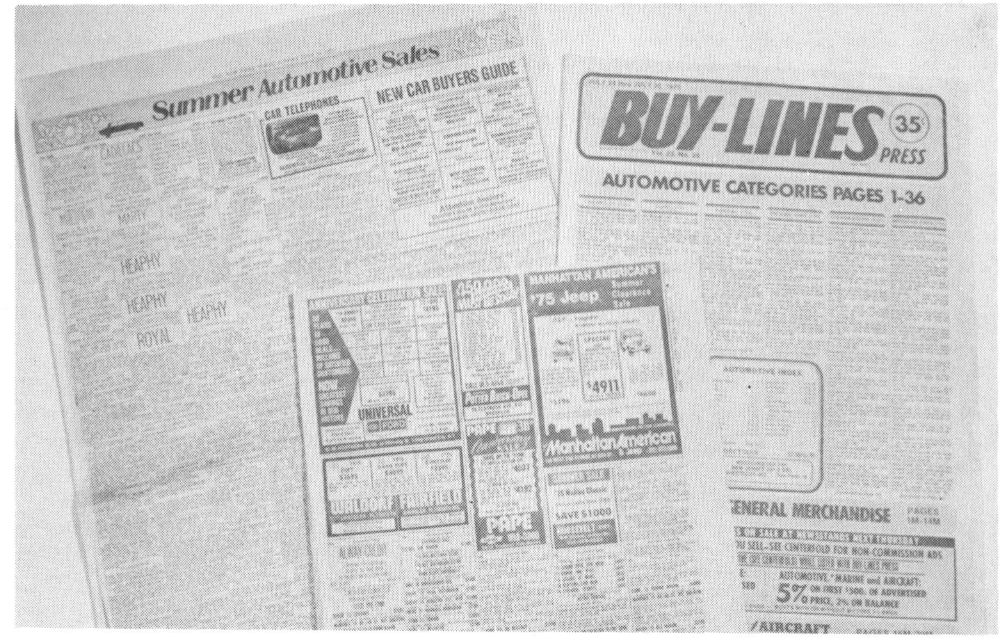

The auto classifieds will tell you the current asking prices of specific used cars.

relative, friend or co-worker, you can end up with an excellent car at an attractive price. Without taking adequate safeguards, buying privately can turn into a nightmarish experience.

Sources of private cars for sale are everywhere. Word of mouth quickly spreads the news. Mention to people that you're in the market for a car and chances are within a very short time someone will tell you that he knows of one for sale. The classified sections of newspapers carry a wealth of used car ads. And the specialized buy and sell weeklies have page after page of cars looking for new owners. Community bulletin boards located in supermarkets, laundromats, etc. usually post one or several notices for cars along with offerings for baby strollers and cribs. You'll find similar notices posted in student lounges and on employee bulletin boards in hospitals and factories. The company house organ might even have space set aside for classified ads. And where there are classifieds, there are used cars for sale.

Then there are the traveling billboards, or the cars riding around with *For Sale* signs posted on them. The advantages of buying privately are obvious. There is no middleman—car dealer—making a profit on the sale. In theory, the seller gets more than he would be offered by a dealer and the buyer pays less.

When you buy privately, you usually can expect to pay somewhere between the car's wholesale and retail value. With an older, less expensive car, the difference between the wholesale and retail value may be only a couple of hundred dollars. Late model luxury cars may have a wholesale/retail price spread up to $1000.

A clean used car sporting a "For Sale" sign has as much impact as a classified ad.

Quick Facts: Where To Find Used Cars

Source	Advantages	Disadvantages
• New car dealer	Better cars Guarantees Good service facilities Late model cars	More expensive May not accept trades
• Glitter lot	Same as new car dealer Best low mileage cars Straightforward dealers	Same as new car dealer Hard to locate Possibly inconvenient locations
• Independent dealer	Competitive prices Accepts trades May try to locate particular car for you if not on hand.	Spotty service Variances in guarantees
• Government auction	Low prices	No guarantees or trades Sporadic schedules You compete with dealers Limited inspection and evaluation
• Commercial auction	Possibly lower prices Regular schedules	Limited inspection and evaluation No guarantees or trades Limited selection Time consuming
• Liquidation auction	Low prices	Sporadic sales Limited selection No guarantees or trades Limited inspection and evaluation
• Consignment seller	Possibly lower prices Nearby locations	No guarantees or trades Possibly no clear title Limited selection
• Private seller	Low price	No guarantees or trades Limited choice—usually one car Widely separated locations Possibly no clear title
• Rental agency	Late model cars Low prices	No guarantees or trades Cars subjected to hard use

That leaves quite a lot of room for price bargaining.

Another advantage of the person-to-person deal is that, in some states, payment of sales tax is avoided. In other states, the two parties may work out an agreement to reduce the amount of sales tax, though not exactly legal, where the sales receipt is made out for substantially less than the actual amount changing hands.

Dealing with another private individual puts you on a more even footing when it comes to bargaining price. The used car salesman is a pro at that game. He does it five or six days a week. And no matter how prepared you are, you're still just an amateur. The private seller is less shrewd than a dealer when it comes to covering up defects.

But buying privately definitely isn't all roses. In fact, the chips probably are stacked against you.

1) The ad may not tell you enough about the car. You may read about just the car you want at just the price you want to pay. When you see the car in person, it may be in top shape inside and out. But you may be violently allergic to the color.

2) The ad may be misleading or downright deceitful. There's no law that requires honesty in classified ads. Good running condition might mean one thing to you. But the seller meant that *you'll* stay in good running condition because you have to push the car to get it started.

3) Unscrupulous dealers will sometimes sneak ads in the private classifieds. If you come across such a dealer, forget about doing business with him as his ethics won't improve during a commercial transaction. Another stunt an underhanded dealer may pull on the private car shopper is to have his salesman take a used car home to sell during the evening or over the weekend.

4) Shady dealers aren't the only pitfall you have to contend with. Private sellers can also be dishonest about their car's history and present state of health. A dealer at least is licensed and your complaint will be heard by the licensing authority. You have no such recourse in a private transaction.

5) You can spend a lot of time and money following up used car ads. The seller usually has one car to offer, and if it doesn't stack up you may have to travel many miles to check out the next seller on your list. It's more convenient to shop a selection of cars at one location than it is to check out individual cars in scattered locations.

6) The primary reason for buying privately is price. But oddly enough, the unwary buyer can stumble into a pitfall here too. The wholesale and retail prices of cars are published in various guides that are available to the public. Often, a private seller will use one of these guides to determine his asking price. The buyer is shown the guidebook price as proof that he's getting a good deal. This would be all well and good, except there are price variances between different guides and these books—revised about every two months—may not accurately reflect the current state of the rapidly changing used car market.

A perfect example is the memorable Arab oil embargo and gasoline shortage. Small economical cars, formerly slow sellers, surged in demand and prices reacted accordingly. At the same time, you could hardly give away the big luxury cars.

1965 LINCOLN Continental 4-door convertible. White top disappears into trunk of rich maroon body with leather seats. Potential classic. Offer reasonable fraction original cost.

Collectors—**1966 CONTINENTAL convertible.** "A" title, full power and tape deck. Excellent condition, owner professional man, low mileage. $3500.

1961 LOTUS Elite Climax Stage II. Tangerine, chrome wire wheels, black glove leather, charcoal wool carpet. Without exaggeration restored to better than new. $3850.

The classified ad method of used car shopping can be time consuming and a letdown.

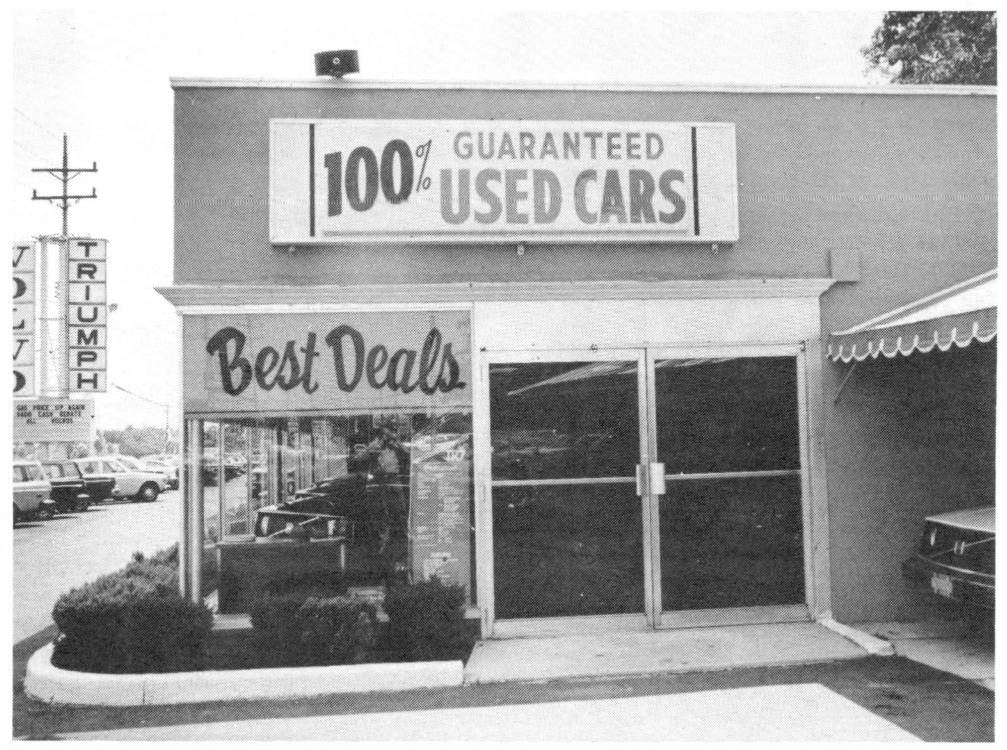

A used car guarantee is only as good as the integrity of the dealer behind the sign.

A couple of months later, and the situation suddenly reversed itself. Dealers use the price guidebooks just as guides. They know which cars are currently hot and can bring substantially more than the book price, and which cars are cold and are selling for much less than the book price. The private buyer and seller may not be aware of current market conditions and may establish a price based on the book. If the car being purchased is currently cold, it's probable that the buyer could have saved a bundle by shopping his local used car dealer instead of purchasing privately.

7) Possibly the worst thing that can happen to the used car buyer is that he purchases a stolen car or one that has a fat payment book that he isn't told about. Forged documents, unfortunately, are commonplace today. So it's up to the buyer to determine that the car isn't stolen or pledged as security for unpaid loans. Demand a clear title or other proof of ownership. If the car turns out to be stolen and is discovered by the police, it is returned to the rightful owner, and you are out your money and out the car. You'll be in the same position if the car is repossessed because the former owner defaulted on his payments or a loan. Dealers usually are bonded against such contingencies so you're protected in the case of a dealer-bought car.

8) Private sellers, as a rule, don't offer guarantees with their cars, so any repairs are strictly your own affair.

9) The same goes for financing. The seller usually wants a cash deal or the bulk of the purchase price on the table. It may be harder for you to swing this type of deal.

10) Wondering what to do with your old car? You don't have the convenience of using it as a trade-in. You'll just have to spend the time selling it to a dealer (at a low price) or switch to the other side of the fence and sell it privately.

How To Shop For A Used Car

Negotiating for a used car has its roots in the system of horse trading.

Before you begin any serious search for a used car, you should have a specific idea of the kind of car you want. Shopping cold at a used car dealer is a bad practice because it puts the salesman in complete control of the situation and allows him to steer you to the cars he wants to sell rather than what may be best suited to your needs.

First off, decide on the general type of car you need. If it's a station car used for short hops back and forth from the train, it's wise to select something small and economical. Likewise, a car that's mainly needed for around town use can be a light, small-engined car with sufficient room for groceries.

For large families, a large car is better suited to reduce fatigue and provide comfort. Larger engines can offer reasonable economy on the highway and provide extra power for hills and passing.

Body styles

Hardtop models traditionally bring the highest prices because their styling is the most popular. They may look more attractive than a boxy sedan, but as a rule will tend to develop rattles sooner. The sedan is the most structurally sound body style because of its extra pillars and posts. Four-door models offer the maximum amount of room.

Convertibles may conjure up visions of youth, but they have several disadvantages. The top provides no barrier to thieves intent on breaking into the car, and vandals crave the sound of ripping fabric. Even under the best conditions, the rear window will require periodic replacement. The ragtop is the most rattle prone body style, suffers from weatherproofing ills and provides no protection in case of a rollover.

A station wagon may be just the thing if you need its room and carrying capacity. Otherwise avoid these models. Wagons tend to see hard use which makes them a bigger risk for potential repair bills. Their long flat-sided shape makes them prone to handling ills in crosswinds. Many are equipped with large engines to handle heavy loads, putting a strain on fuel economy. They also are rattle prone. A good rule of thumb is to select the simplest and smallest car that will suit your needs. The smaller cars are less expensive to operate and maintain, and do not suffer the initial heavy depreciation of larger cars.

Make and model

Brand loyalty is common to many car buyers. Chevys, Buicks or Fords often run in a family. With a car that's a couple of years old, make is not as important as condition or price. You may be turned off by a car's styling or dashboard layout. But chances are, you can expect comparable transportation from a used Ford or a used Chevy in like condition.

While different makes and models often provide comparable transportation, there may be wide fluctuations in the price. Some cars just weren't right for their time when they were introduced, the most notable example being the Edsel. They didn't sell well and consequently fetch lower prices on the used car market. Car lines that are discontinued, such as the Ford Falcon, also tend to slump in value. The Edsel and the Falcon both provided reliable transportation on a par with other cars in their class. But they are generally priced lower on the used car market.

If you're worried about obtaining parts for discontinued models, keep in mind that manufacturers are required to make parts for their models for seven years. Often parts on discontinued lines will be interchangeable with some of those on current models.

Some manufacturer's products have a poorer image than others. On the other hand, expect to pay more for popular cars or sporty styled cars.

Some imported cars will also lose value more quickly than comparable domestic models. But balance price against availability of service. Domestic cars generally have a service advantage over the imports.

Recalls

Cars recalled by the manufacturer may not all have the suspected safety defect. It's also possible that a previous owner had the defect corrected.

Cars that were not well received when new very often become bargains when used.

You can check whether a particular car was recalled by calling the manufacturer's District Service Manager. He's listed in the car's owner's manual. Or a new car dealer of that make can tell you who he is. Be prepared to tell the District Service Manager the car's model, year and the vehicle identification number—found on a metal tag attached to the door frame on top of the dashboard or on the firewall.

If you're the independent type and don't mind driving a car that is not currently in vogue with the masses, you can save a heap of money. The Edsel, interestingly enough, is now in demand by collectors and actually is appreciating in value.

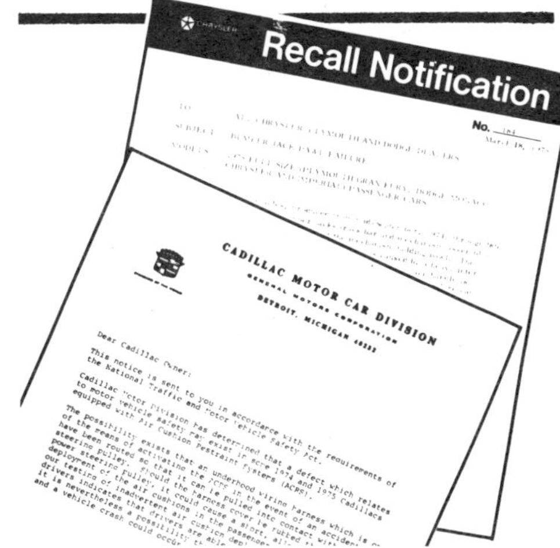

Was a used car involved in a recall? Check with the District Service Manager.

Age and depreciation

How old is too old? Assuming you are looking at cars in average condition with normal mileage accumulation, you should weigh the car's depreciation cycle in your decision. Cars do not all depreciate at the same rate. Some drop in value relatively quickly, while others hold their value relatively well. Price spreads between cars having different rates of depreciation tend to diminish as they become older.

If you intend to buy a used car every year or so, select one having a slow rate of depreciation. That way you won't take a beating at trade-in time.

The new car buyer suffers the most on depreciation. The first year is always the most severe in value loss. As a rule, the more recent model year car is always more desirable. A car that is two years old is considered optimum because it may have depreciated to one-half its original price, while traveling only one-fifth its useful life's mileage.

Car's track record

At this point you should have narrowed your selection of a used car to several models and years. A little research at this point will help to further focus your decision. Check with your local library for back issues of consumer and automotive magazines that carry road tests and evaluations of the cars you have in mind. Get the experts' opinion. Some of these magazines feature owner's reports that reveal potential long range problems.

Check with other owners of the cars you are considering. Ask them specific questions as to gas mileage, mechanical difficulties, etc. rather than a general "How do you like your car?"

When to shop

The less pressure you're under to buy a car, the better your chances of getting a good deal. The best times to peruse the used car lots are late fall and winter. The dealers have a bountiful supply of used cars at this time resulting from trade-ins on new models. Winter traditionally is a slow car selling season, so dealers are anxious

To find out how your car was rated when new, check back issues of auto magazines.

for business. Some states tax a dealer on the cars he has in stock at the end of the year. Dealers are therefore anxious to convert inventory into cash to reduce the tax bite.

The end of the year is also the time when many dealer sales contests for their salesmen draw to a close. The salesmen may be particularly eager to deal in order to meet a sales quota or increase a bonus. Another time salesmen feel generous is during or right after a nasty weather spell. Customer traffic is down at this time and the silver-tongued set tries to make up for lost sales.

Spring and early summer are times when used car sales are strong, so expect to pay more in a seller's market.

How much should it cost?

Before you start out on your shopping tour, get an idea of how much the particular car you've selected is selling for.

There are several used car price guides available. But the best are the guides put out by the National Automobile Dealers Association (NADA) and the Kelly Blue Book. These guides list imported and domestic cars by make, model and year and show the wholesale value, retail price and the average loan price or the amount that can be financed. They also tell the dealer how much money to add to a car's wholesale and retail price for various options, such as air conditioning. These guides may be hard to obtain as they're sold primarily by subscription and not on newsstands.

Banks and lending institutions use similar guides and you can find out the car's book value just by seeking preliminary loan information.

There is one guide that is sold on newsstands and is relatively easy to obtain. It's called *Edmund's Used Car Prices* and is a compilation of prices from other trade pricing guides. There are four issues a year and prices are updated quarterly.

The book value is just an indication, *not* the final word, on a car's worth. The prices are compiled from information on thousands of wholesale and retail transactions. There is a time lag between obtaining the information and distributing the published guide. So it's possible for portions of the guide to be obsolete, especially just before a revised edition is released.

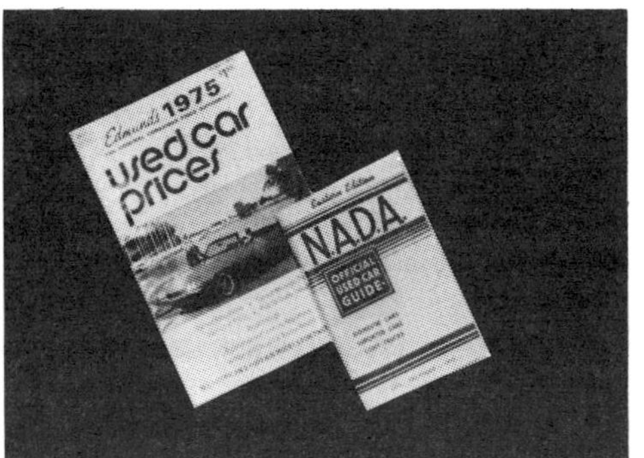

The classifieds

Checking the classified ads is another way to determine current market prices. You'll have to read the ads carefully to learn what options are included and tipoffs to condition. Terms like "needs work" or "good transportation" could mean serious mechanical or cosmetic defects.

Don't be misled by liberal use of the word "cream puff." There is actually no standard of quality for the use of the word. So a seller is free to use it on anything from a car that really is in like-new, showroom condition to a real clapped out clunker. When checking classifieds, remember, these are asking prices, not final prices.

If you intend buying privately, you'll need to obtain more information over the phone as classified ads rarely tell the whole story. Try to get a complete picture of the car before you invest time and money for a visit. Speak to the person who actually is selling the car. Often, another person in the household will try to be helpful in answering your questions but doesn't really know the facts. Call back if you have to. Realize that you may not be getting the truth over the phone or in person for that matter. If you ask an owner why he's selling the car, don't expect him to say, "because the engine and transmission are about to fall out" even if that's the case.

Used car price guides may or may not tell current prices depending on market shifts. But they do give you a fairly good general idea of what a particular model is selling for.

pontiac

Year Model Body Type	Original List Price	Current Average Wholesale	Retail
4 Door 3 St Wgn	4542	1775	2250
BONNEVILLE 8			
4 Door Hardtop	4354	1725	2200
2 Door Hardtop	4287	1725	2200
4 Door Sedan	4225	1650	2125
GRAND SAFARI 8			
4 Door 2 St Wgn	4748	1875	2375
4 Door 3 St Wgn	4895	1950	2450
GRAND VILLE 8			
2 Door Hardtop	4586	1775	2250
4 Door Hardtop	4654	1775	2250
2 Door Convertible	4828	1700	2175
GRAND PRIX 8			

Year Model Body Type	Original List Price	Current Average Wholesale	Retail
2 Door Hdtp Coupe	3203	1350	1775
4 Door Sedan	3166	1275	1700
2 Dr Spt Convertible	3580	1300	1725
4 Dr 2 St Wagon	3623	1450	1875
4 Dr 3 St Wagon	3730	1500	1950
FIREBIRD 6•			
2 Door Hardtop	3201	1625	2100
• For 8 cylinder models add $100 wholesale and $125 retail.			
VENTURA II 6•			
2 Door Coupe	2660	1300	1725
4 Door Sedan	2688	1275	1700
• For 8 cylinder models add $80			

Quick Facts: Common Ad Abbreviations

a/c — *air conditioning*
acc — *accessories*
all discs — *4-wheel disc brakes*
AM/FM — *AM/FM radio*
auto (or AT) — *automatic transmission*
conv — *convertible*
cpe — *coupe*
crm puf — *cream puff*
cyl — *cylinders*
def — *defogger*
discs — *disc brakes (on front wheels only)*
dlr — *dealer*
dr — *door*
fac — *factory installed*
F/BK — *fastback*
full power — *power steering, power brakes and power windows*
gar — *garaged*
h — *heater*
HT — *hardtop*
int — *interior*
lthr — *leather*
lo — *low*
mags — *special custom wheels*
man — *manual transmission*
pb — *power brakes*
p disc — *power disc brakes (front only)*
pw — *power windows*
r — *radio*
radials — *radial tires*
reblt — *rebuilt*
sed — *sedan*
snows — *snow tires*
spd — *speed*
ss — *stick shift*
tape — *tape deck*
trans (also tr) — *transmission*
v/rf — *vinyl roof*
warr — *warranty*
wgn — *wagon*
ww — *whitewall tires*

Dealer ads

Dealer ads are another story. They can sometimes read almost as if the dealer will give you a car just for walking in the door. Common sense will tell you that a dealer is in business to make money and not for the sheer fun of being a good guy in a white hat or making singing commercials on TV. His salesmen have to eat too, and they get paid a commission on the profit their sale brings the dealer.

Many of these ads sound real tempting, but actually do not give you any information about the cars or their condition. Terms like "We will not be undersold" or "No down payment" are meaningless. It's impossible for a dealer to be undersold on a used car no matter what the price, because no one else has that particular used car. The "no down payment" may be true. But the ad doesn't say that your trade-in will be used in lieu of cash. "Money Back If Not Satisfied" sounds pretty straightforward. But like most things that sound too good, you can bet on catches like the offer holding for only a 24-hour time period and a healthy service charge written into the fine print. Or the ad might offer repossessed cars for a small down payment and low payments. Of course, the ad doesn't mention any of the additional charges the dealer tacks on for work he did to put the car back in shape, like new tires, battery, etc.

Some ads are designed merely to generate traffic on the dealer's lot and keep the salesmen busy. Avoid dealers that use obvious come-ons in their advertising. A straightforward ad describing the cars usually in glowing terms is a good indication, but not a guarantee, of a straightforward dealer.

How to shop

With some idea of the market price for the car you want, do some rough calculating on your finances. If you plan to buy on time, figure at least a 30% down payment and allow a conservative estimate for your car if you plan to trade.

This is a ballpark way of estimating if you can swing a deal on the car you want. Don't forget to allow for incidentals like sales tax and registration fees.

Visit three or four reputable dealers. If you're following up an ad for a specific car and the salesman tries to steer you to a more expensive car, you are the victim of a "bait and switch" routine, and it pays to shop elsewhere.

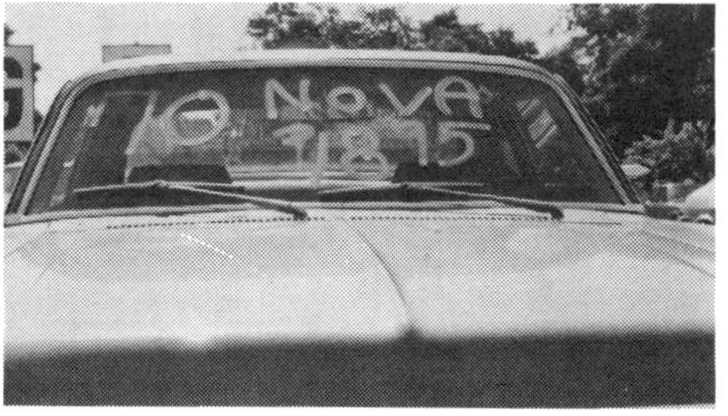

Some used car lots mark prices right on windshields. But it still pays to haggle.

Tell the salesman what you're looking for and what you want to spend. Also mention that the condition of the car is more important to you than its price. Say that you're shopping at this point but you intend to buy within two days. Ask prices of the cars he shows you but don't attempt to negotiate at this point. Take into account that his initial quote will be high and that he will come down when the discussion gets serious.

When visiting a dealer, park your car one or two blocks away so the salesman cannot see it and estimate its trade-in worth. By telling the salesman that you're shopping, you should be able to avoid a sales pitch and check the cars out in relative peace. You also are alerting him to the fact that he will have to be competitive in his final price. Don't get taken in by the phrase that the car is x dollars if you buy immediately. He'll be as happy to make the sale tomorrow as he is today.

Dealers will use all sorts of methods to increase their lot traffic.

When you walk onto a lot, don't head straight for the car of your dreams even if it's sitting there in the exact color you want. You're telegraphing to a perceptive salesman that you're in love with one of his cars. If this happens, forget about some of your bargaining power. Instead, look over a couple of other cars first before heading for your dream machine. This way, the salesman won't know which car you're really interested in.

By the same token, don't tell the salesman how great a car looks and how you'd like to own it. He'd love to own your bank account. Try to be noncommittal if he asks what you think of a car he shows you.

Be noncommittal if the salesman questions you about a trade-in. Tell him you're considering selling privately. You can always change your mind. You'll have better bargaining leverage if you introduce your trade-in after hearing his bottom cash price.

Don't let the salesman show you cars out of your price range. There's more profit for the dealer and a larger commission for the salesman on more expensive cars. Realize that the higher the price the more attractive the car. But you have to draw the line somewhere.

Be careful about leaving deposits. They may not be refundable.

Once you've lined up the cars you like, it's time to thoroughly check out their condition.

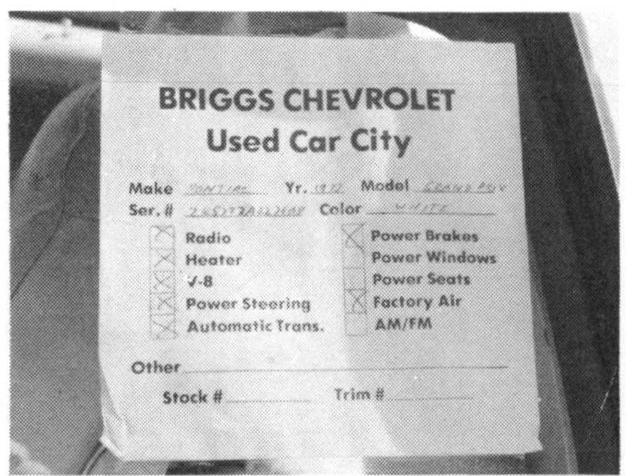

Identifying options and accessories makes it easy for the buyer to screen cars.

Quick Facts: Reading Between The Lines On The Used Car Ads

ACME MOTORS GUARANTEES LOWEST PRICES
Lowest prices of what? Floor mats? No two used cars are exactly alike because of differences in use, driver habits and maintenance. So no one else can compete on price for that particular car. What are the conditions of "guarantee?"

FREE 5-YEAR WARRANTY ON PARTS & LABOR
If you have all your service performed at the dealer, only certain items are covered by the warranty. And you must have regular routine maintenance performed by dealer at exhorbitant prices.

SORRY, PRICES ARE SO LOW WE ARE UNABLE TO MENTION THEM
Who's stopping them? Prices are low on certain cars you wouldn't be seen dead in. Bargain-priced cars have all been sold.

BELOW COST
Whose cost? Below original sticker price? Dealers can't stay in business if they sell cars for less than they pay for them.

$500 REBATE
If you buy the car at the windshield price. Chances are, you could bargain more off the price without rebate.

MONEY BACK IF NOT SATISFIED
Offer good for 24 hours and you have to pay a "service charge" that amounts to more than renting a car for 24 hours.

NO DOWN PAYMENT
Your trade-in is an acceptable substitute.

SMALL DEPOSIT HOLDS ANY CAR
The deposit is not refundable.

Checking Out A Used Car

Cars on used car lots often look too good to be used. They've been detailed.

Detailing used cars

If you're car shopping at your friendly neighborhood used car lot, you'll notice something interesting. All or most of the cars look too new to be used. They sparkle and shine and may hardly show any signs of wear at all. They'll even smell new. That's because the cars have been detailed, which in the trade means reconditioned.

Detailing is used to mask a car's previous history. What the dealer invests to correct or cover up defects, he gets back many times over from the new owner.

Almost every car on the lot has been detailed to some degree. The dealer has either his own people do the job or he farms the car out to detailing specialists who serve all the used car dealers in the area. The car may pass through the hands of several detailers—all specialists—before it's placed under the spotlights and plastered with banners reading "one owner car" or "A-1."

The dealer can have this work done much cheaper than you can, because he pays wholesale prices. He also offsets some of his costs by estimating how much detailing is required when the car is traded in and adjusts his offer accordingly.

Tricks of the trade

The first thing a dealer does to a trade-in is go over it mechanically. The good dealers will correct defects and problems. This might involve anything from rebuilding the transmission, replacing worn mufflers and brakes to tuning the engine and aligning the front end.

Shady dealers will try to hide the defects rather than correct them. This is the man who uses that infamous recipe of pouring sawdust into standard transmissions to cover up noises caused by worn parts. Nowadays, heavy grease is used to mask the sound of worn gears and bearings. He'll "cure" a cracked engine block with a healthy dose of radiator stop leak—a temporary measure at best—and slap on a set of cheap recapped tires to hide an alignment problem, or even worse, a bent frame.

After the mechanical problems are dealt with, one way or another, the car goes through a cosmetic transformation. Steam cleaning is first on the agenda. The engine compartment, block, fender wells and even the trunk may receive the Mr. Clean treatment. The engine is repainted the original color and the engine decals are replaced or rubbed with Vaseline to make them look new. Still in the engine compartment, the firewall and the radiator are repainted and the battery is cleaned and then sprayed with clear lacquer.

The interior is next to be renewed. The headliner may be redyed or a new one installed. The old headliner may be worn, stained or may have had telltale holes indicating use as a taxi. Vinyl seats are spray painted, as is the dashboard. The whole interior is cleaned with a deodorizing shampoo. Worn carpets may be spray painted, touched up in worn areas or replaced with new carpeting or cheaper rubber mats.

Tired upholstery benefits from a set of seatcovers and worn armrests and floor pedal rubbers are replaced. The trunk may receive special treatment. It is hand cleaned, scratches and scars are repainted and the trunk mat replaced. All tires are repainted. The exterior will receive corrective bodywork, paint touch-ups and the mandatory rotary buffer wax job.

A glass specialist replaces any cracked windows and a lot man replaces items like cracked lenses, burned out bulbs and missing lighters, hubcaps or chrome trim. The interior is then given a blast of "new car" fragrance from a spray can. The whole detailing job usually is effective enough to bluff the average used car buyer. But the shopper who knows where to look can pick up the clues left behind by the detailers.

Condition of the interior can be a good clue to a car's overall condition.

A sharp interior may be the result of lavish attention by the owner, or detailing.

Initial inspection

The best time to closely examine a car is in strong daylight. Everything looks great at night under a dealer's bright floodlights. Rain can add to a paint's sheen and helps some engines to run better than they would on a dry day. Since you'll want to peek underneath the car, wear clothes that you won't mind getting soiled, and bring along a flashlight.

The initial inspection is a screening technique to weed out questionable or obviously unsound cars. If a car passes your inspection the next stop is to have it thoroughly checked by a mechanic or diagnostic center. If a dealer or private party refuses to let your mechanic look over the car, walk away.

The initial inspection is a systematic approach to evaluating the car's exterior, interior and mechanical systems. The key here is to be organized and methodical in

Stand back a few feet and slowly walk around the car. Does it seem to sag?

Body rust often will show up as small spots or pits next to chrome body trim.

Sighting along body panels can uncover telltale clues of a past accident.

your inspection and not jump from the trunk to the headlights to the engine oil.

Your inspection should take a double approach. You are looking for evidence of serious damage, which should immediately disqualify the car, and minor or cosmetic deficiencies which you may be able to use as a lever when negotiating price. Signs that a car has been detailed or reconditioned should not be the sole grounds for disqualifying a car. But they should be noted for later, more intensive checking by you or your mechanic as to the car's actual state of health.

The exterior

Stand a few feet back from the car and walk around it slowly. You're looking for an overall impression and clues to possible problems. Does the car seem to sag if it's on level ground? If so, you can count on a suspension problem. Does the paint appear evenly matched? Are the bumpers straight and do they appear evenly aged with the rest of the chrome? New bumpers could mean replacement due to an accident and door handles that don't appear uniform might indicate an entire door was replaced for the same reason.

Now step in for a close look. Sight along the sides of the body for ripples or unevenness in the sheet metal—evidence that the car has seen bodywork. Open the doors and sight along the drip rails at the top of the car. Crooked drip rails are also evidence of damage. Check for signs of repainting. A late model car shouldn't need repainting for at least three years. Reasons for earlier repainting include accident damage and rust. If the chrome, bumpers and grille are pitted with rust and the paint looks shiny-new, you can bet the car has a bad rust problem or was in an accident. Rust usually starts in hidden areas like the wheelwells and rocker panels. Check out these areas thoroughly, especially for bumps under the paint. Another favorite place for rust to start is behind chrome strips on the body. Try to slide the strip slightly and note whether the paint behind the strip matches the rest of the car. It may not be exact because it hasn't been aged by the sun, but it should be close. Probe the metal behind or around the strip gently with a nail file. Soft spots indicate rust. Use the same procedure on the bottom of the rocker panels. The rocker panels are the areas below the doors. The inside edges on the bottom of the doors and the lower fender edges should also be looked at for signs of rust.

If you can push your fingernail or the point of a nail file through any areas of the body, it indicates that rust has gained a strong foothold and it could be an expensive proposition to eliminate.

Telltale signs of repainting are slight traces of paint on weatherstripping, glass or chrome. Open the hood and inspect the firewall. Do the wires show traces of paint? What about the paint underneath the wires? Does it match the rest of the car? Doorjambs are another area to check for signs of repainting.

Next, turn your attention to the doors. They should open and close smoothly and easily and fit snugly and evenly when shut. Hold the door handle button in and close the door. If it is difficult to close, the door could be sprung, indicating a past accident. Open the door and check it for sagging, indicating hard use. Also check the hood and trunk lid for proper fit and alignment.

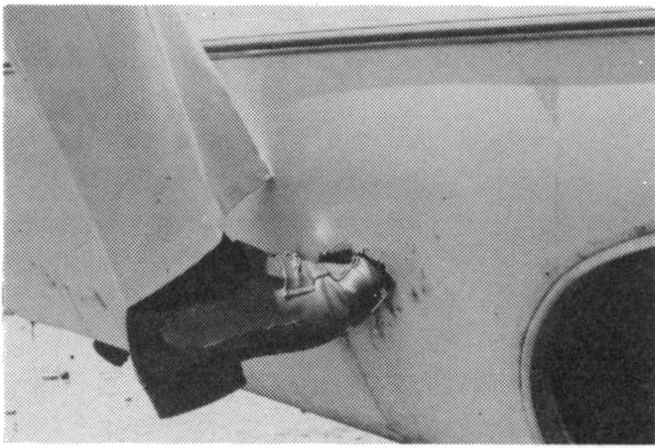

If you're able to poke something through a body panel, rust is excessive. Forget the car.

Under the car

If you've brought your trusty flashlight, you can note obvious conditions under the car. This is a preliminary inspection, the final one being done by your own mechanic with the car on a lift.

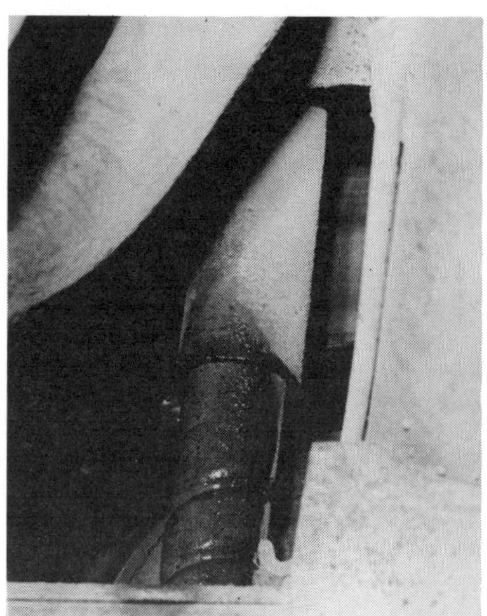

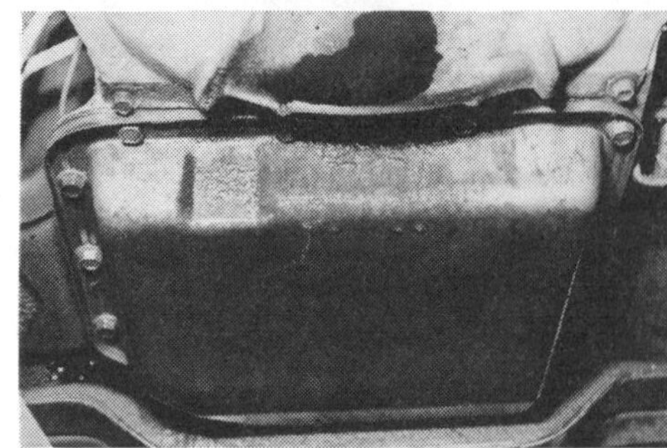

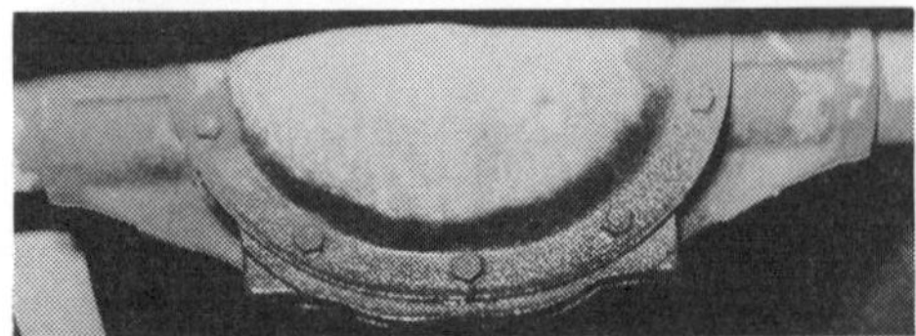

Underneath the car, check for leaky shocks (top), transmission (center) and rear end (bottom).

Note the condition of the exhaust system. If the muffler and pipes appear extremely rusty, you have some replacement expenses ahead of you. If sections of the frame appear cleaner than others, or are freshly painted, it's likely that major structural repairs have been done and you should reject the car. Look at the inside of each wheel. Signs of leaks mean faulty wheel cylinders or damaged brake lines. Check the ground for signs of leaks. These could be engine oil, transmission grease (standard transmission) automatic transmission fluid, radiator coolant, brake fluid, rear end grease or even gasoline.

While you're close to the ground, note the condition of the tires. Check the tread depth with a dime. If you can see the date, expect to shell out for replacements.

Wear old clothes and don't be afraid to get down on the ground to check the car.

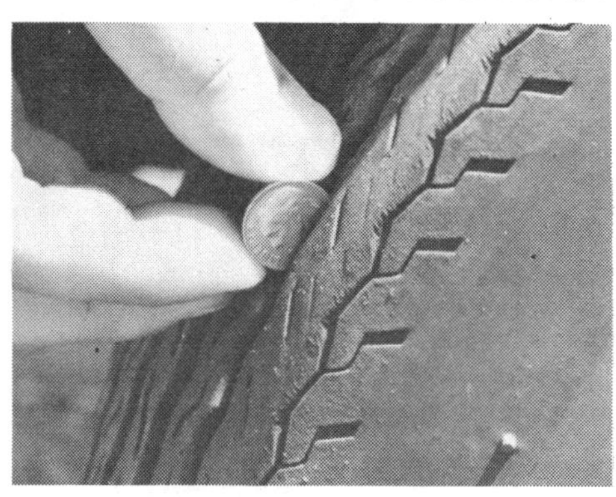

A quick way to determine adequate tire tread is to insert a dime in a groove.

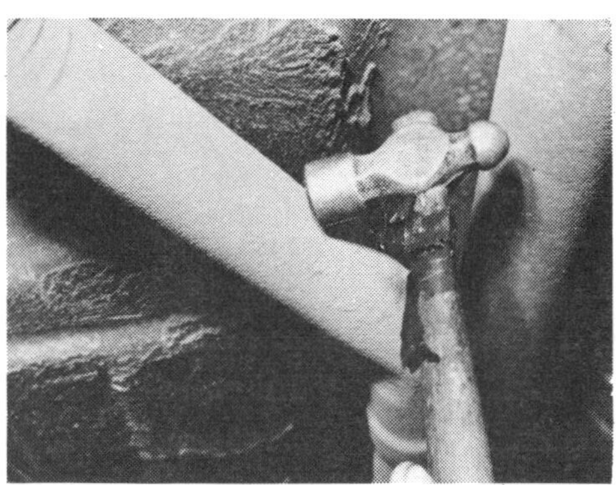

Tapping exhaust pipes with a hammer can reveal problems such as rust.

Interior inspection

The interior of a privately owned car is more likely to be a true reflection of the car's overall condition than the interior of a dealer's car. If the present owner didn't at least make an effort to clean up the interior prior to sale, you can bet that he's fallen down on maintenance. Does the car's interior condition jibe with the mileage indicated on the odometer? At one time turning back the clock was common practice. Today, with federal laws against such tampering, reducing the numbers is less prevalent but not entirely eliminated. The average mileage for a car is between 10,000-12,000 miles per year. A car one or two years old should show light to moderate wear on the pedal pads. If the pads are excessively worn or are brand new, suspect higher than average mileage. Other indications of actual mileage are old lubrication stickers on door jambs, amount of wear on floor mats and condition of upholstery.

If everything looks too new the car probably has been detailed. Evidence of this is a trace of paint overspray on the metal doorstep plate. If the dash has been repainted, you might find tinges of color on the radio buttons or interior trim. Bounce on the seats. They should offer firm support. A sagging driver's seat indicates high mileage or hard use. New seat covers may be hiding worn upholstery. If the rear seats are worn more than the front, the car may have been used as a taxi. Check under and around the dash for any unusual holes which may also indicate a taxi background.

Keys that fit loosely in the ignition switch can be the result of excessive wear and high mileage. If there are more than two separate keys needed to open the various locks (ignition, door, glove compartment and trunk) suspect that the car may have been stolen at one time and the original lock(s) damaged as a result.

Other high mileage indicators are a worn steering wheel rim and a frayed armrest.

Sit behind the wheel. With the engine off, press the accelerator and brake pedals a few times. Pedals that feel loose or sloppy are probably worn because of high mileage no matter what the pedal pads indicate. And while you're behind the wheel, make sure that there are no instruments or accessories that have obviously been removed.

Check out all of the systems and the accessories including windshield washers and wipers—listen for quiet operation—radio, all the lights and directional signals, power windows and seats if applicable, etc. The engine may have to be running to check out items like the air conditioner and power accessories.

Excessively low mileage is not desirable either. A car subjected to local stop and go driving for short periods may be in worse mechanical shape than a car with more than average highway miles under its wheels.

Continue your interior inspection by opening and closing all the windows. They should work smoothly and not bind. Check for leaks around all windows including the windshield and rear window. Weatherstripping should fit snugly against the glass. Otherwise you'll hear a wind whistle at highway speeds.

If the ignition key fits sloppily, it can indicate very high mileage.

Be sure to try all the switches and controls to make sure they all are operable.

Dangling or loose wires under the dashboard are a sign of past and present problems.

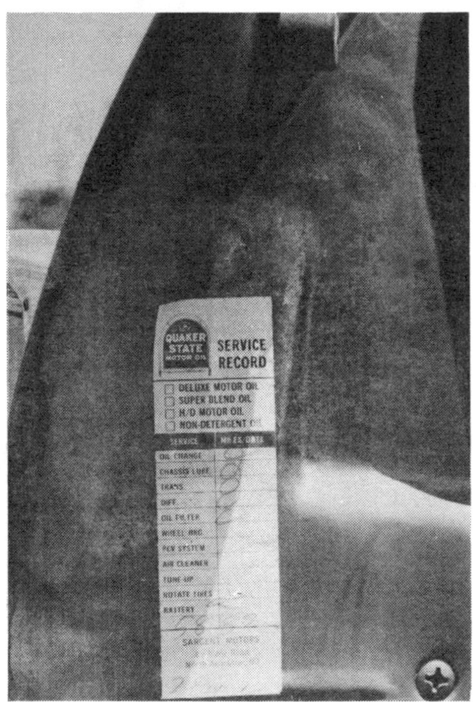

Lubrication stickers can tell the story of proper maintenance and actual mileage.

Another indication of actual mileage is the amount of wear on the brake pedal pad.

Loose or damaged weatherstripping around windows will cause wind whistle at speed.

Mechanical inspection

A complete mechanical evaluation requires visually inspecting various mechanical systems and an operational check which involves a road test. If a dealer or private party won't let you road test a car, your best bet is to look elsewhere. Otherwise you're opening yourself up for too many unhappy surprises.

If the engine is excessively dirty, it pays to have it steam cleaned in order to more easily spot leaks. Visible signs of oil or coolant leaks can mean only a heater hose needs tightening or, more seriously, a damaged engine block.

Inspect the radiator. Dampness or greenish stains on the core is a sign of seepage. Silver spots on the core mean that leaks have been repaired with white lead. With the engine cold, remove the radiator cap and feel around inside the neck. An appreciable accumulation of gunk is a tipoff to cooling system problems.

Check the engine oil by removing the dipstick. If the oil is very thick or gummy, or it has a grayish color, it's being used to mask an engine problem like burning oil or to quiet worn bearings. Unless you're game for a major engine overhaul the car is not for you. While you've got the dipstick out, take a close look at how shiny it is. A car with more than 10,000 miles will have a dull gray or even black dipstick. A shiny, new looking stick means that it was either replaced with a new one, or, the old one was given the steel wool treatment. An oil change usually accompanies the steel wool treatment so that an examination gives the impression of an internally clean engine. In fact, the complete opposite might be true. Inspect the wiring. Badly frayed wires, especially on the firewall, are an expensive replacement proposition.

A strong odor of gasoline under the hood or under the car means there's a leak and a potential fire hazard from a defective gas line, fuel pump or carburetor. Exception: flooded carburetor.

Get ready to start the engine. With the ignition switch in the On position, most of the dashboard engine warning lights should be on. The remainder, including the temperature warning light, should glow when the key is advanced to the Start position.

The starter should spin the motor rapidly with no unusual noises, and the engine should fire up quickly. A slow cranking engine means a weak battery, poor terminal connections or a bad starter. An engine that takes a long time to start might need a simple choke adjustment, a tuneup, a major overhaul—or anything in between.

When the engine starts, all the engine warning lights should go out. If they don't, the car has problems that require a mechanic's attention. If the "Gen", "Alt" or "Bat" light remains on while the engine is running, the problem could range anywhere from a disconnected wire to a bad alternator and regulator.

Listen for any knocking, slapping or loud tapping sounds. They indicate potentially serious engine problems. If you hear a light ticking sound, it probably is a sticking valve lifter—a problem that can sometimes be cured with a good detergent oil. Any noises should diminish as the engine warms up. Hissing or loud muffler sounds mean leaks somewhere in the exhaust system and can originate at deteriorated gaskets or a rusted out pipe. It is all right for an engine to idle rapidly when it is warming up. But you should be able to slow the idle down by tapping the accelerator when the engine is warm.

If the engine continues to run at a faster than normal idle speed, request that the owner or salesman slow it down. Or if you can, do it yourself. A fast idle may be a coverup for an engine that stalls rapidly or has more serious problems.

The engine should idle smoothly, evenly and quietly. You can check the engine smoothness by placing your hand an inch or so away from the exhaust pipe. The power pulses should be evenly spaced and regular. A periodic miss or burp can mean valve or ignition problems.

While you're standing at the rear of the car, have the seller race the engine a few times. Blue smoke coming from the

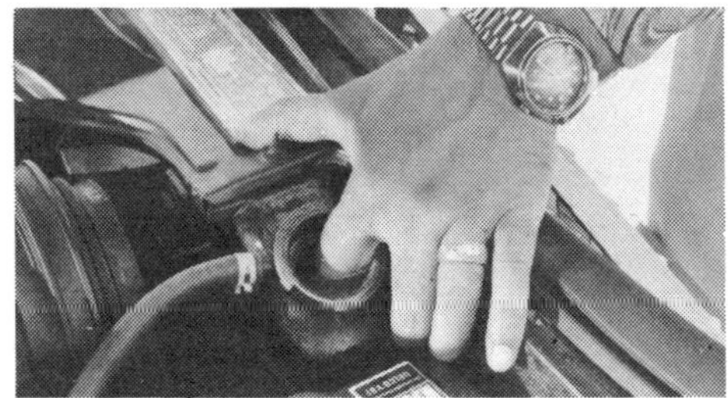

Check the condition of the radiator by feeling for gunk at the filler neck.

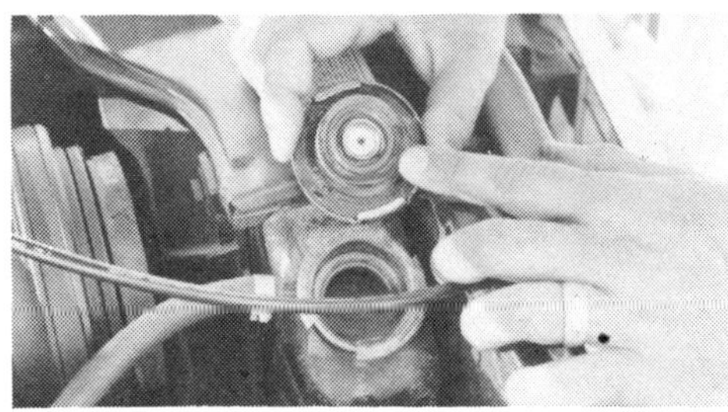

The radiator cap also may show evidence of a stop-leak used to mask a leaky condition.

The condition of the engine oil is most important. But it may have just been changed.

The carburetor and fuel system should be inspected thoroughly for proper operation and safety.

exhaust indicates the car is burning oil. Black smoke indicates a carburetor adjustment is in order. Water vapor is normal when the engine is cold. If you see heavy white vapor when the engine is warm, be suspicious of serious engine damage.

Additional evidence that the engine is burning oil is a deposit of thick black gunk inside the tailpipe.

If the car has power brakes or power steering, test their operation while the engine is idling. Non-power brakes and steering can be checked with the engine either on or off.

To test the brakes, push the pedal down slowly without pumping. It should not sink too close to the floor and it should feel firm, not spongy. Hold the pedal depressed for about one minute. If it starts to sink further, there is a problem with the brakes, most likely the master cylinder.

To check the steering, turn the wheels in the straight ahead position and determine the amount of play in the system by turning the wheel lightly from side to side until resistance is felt. There should be under two inches of wheel play. Sometimes when a car is equipped with power steering, it's difficult to tell where the play ends and front wheel movement begins. In that case, stand outside the car and move the steering wheel through the open driver's window while you watch the front wheels for movement.

Place the car in gear and inch forward slowly at the same time turning the steering wheel all the way from lock to lock. There should be no binding or tight spots in the wheel travel—an indication of overtightened steering adjustments to compensate for wear. There shouldn't be any clunks or strange sounds either. Groans or squeaks from power steering cars can mean anything from a low fluid level or a loose belt to fluid leaks and a malfunctioning power steering pump. Another steering check involves grabbing the top of each front wheel and shaking back and forth as hard as you can. Movement or clunking sounds spell front end trouble.

Unevenly worn tread, felt by running

The pulse at the exhaust pipe can indicate an engine's state of health and tune.

You can get a rough idea of wheel alignment problems by sighting from the front.

To check the play in the steering system, watch the front wheels for small movement.

Uneven or unusual tire wear is an indication of wheel alignment or other problems.

your hand across the face of the tire to feel feather edges you sometimes can't see, are sure tipoffs to alignment or balancing problems. If the front tires appear new, stand about 15 feet in front of the car, stoop down and look at the front wheels. If they appear to slant in at the top or bottom, the alignment is out of adjustment.

Back to the engine. Check for leaks again, this time with the engine running. Also peek under the car for oil or transmission fluid seepage. With the engine warm and running, check the automatic transmission fluid. The normal color is usually reddish. If the fluid appears brownish, bring the dipstick to your nose and give it the smell test. Fluid that has a burned smell indicates a transmission problem like slipping clutches. Low transmission fluid can mean leaks caused by worn seals.

Turn off the engine and check the power steering fluid level. Here again, a low level can indicate leaks in the system.

Next, stop and start the engine five consecutive times. The engine should fire up instantly every time when warm. Avoid pumping the gas pedal which can easily flood the engine.

Check the automatic transmission by shifting it through all the gear positions with your foot held firmly on the brake pedal. There should be no groans, whines or jerks. Shift back and forth from Drive to Reverse a few times. The gears should engage smoothly and silently without hesitation. Any clunks are telling you of driveline play or worn universal joints.

A preliminary suspension check can be made by pushing down hard on each corner of the car. There should be no squeaks or other noises. The car should bounce once and then stop. Otherwise, the shock absorbers are bad.

Road test

The road test is an essential part of the evaluation program. Insist on it even if it means disqualifying the car.

During the test you should concentrate on two things. First, the overall impression or feel of the car. If the car doesn't leave you with a good impression even though you can't say specifically why, don't buy it. Second, the road test should give you a fairly good evaluation of the individual system.

Try to find a variety of driving conditions that include a steep hill, sharp turns, an uncrowded highway and a bumpy section of road. Prior to road testing make sure all the tires are properly and equally inflated.

Engine and transmission

The engine should operate smoothly and quietly at all speeds. On a clear section of highway or a deserted street, apply full power from a standing start. There should be no hesitation in the flow of power, no excessive smoke from the exhaust nor loud pinging or other noises. The automatic transmission should not slip under full power or allow the engine to race between shifts. Accelerate to 55 mph and then, with your foot off the accelerator, coast back down to 20 mph. Then apply full power once again. Check once more for exhaust smoke and notice if the transmission downshifts smoothly and promptly into the kickdown gear. Reduce speed once more to about 15 mph and accelerate briskly to about 40 mph without engaging the kickdown gear. The engine should pull smoothly without hesitating or bucking—both are indications of possible valve or carburetion problems.

Reduce speed and shift the transmission into low range—second gear with a standard transmission—and accelerate up to 40 mph. The engine should pull evenly at this speed without missing or hesitating and should not have loud tapping or knocking sounds. Placing a heavy load on the engine will reveal possible bearing problems. To do this, accelerate the car to 15 mph and maintain that speed with the brake while slowly depressing the accelerator to the floor. This test should be conducted for only a brief period. Any bearing noise that you hear should have an even rhythm. An irregular beat should disqualify the car. Any other strange or loud sounds should be discussed with your mechanic.

If you can locate a steep hill, reduce the car's speed to about 20 mph and then accelerate briskly to 40 mph. The engine should not protest by missing, bucking or hammering.

Check the automatic transmission shifting operation under normal driving conditions. From a standing start under moderate acceleration, the shifts should be silent and almost unnoticeable. Stopping from normal driving speeds should not produce any noticeable shifts or clunks from the transmission.

If the car has a manual transmission, check that the gears engage smoothly and silently and that the clutch action is even and not grabby. The clutch pedal should not be unduly stiff or have more than two inches of play at either end of its travel.

Check for clutch slipping by firmly applying the parking brake and engaging high gear. Depress the accelerator to race the engine slightly and let the clutch out slowly. The engine should stall out smoothly if the clutch is in good working order.

Brakes

The parking brake should hold the car firmly on a hill or against light accelerator pressure with the car in gear. Test the service brakes first at low speed, about 15-20 mph, on a clear and level road by maintaining light pressure on the steering wheel and applying the brakes hard. The car should not swerve. All four brakes should exert equal force. If one or two wheels lock up, grab or squeal, expect to spend some money replacing brake linings or doing other brake work. The pedal should remain firm and not sink closer than two inches from the floor. A low pedal can mean anything from a simple brake adjustment to more expensive repairs.

On a clear section of roadway make four hard consecutive stops from 55 mph. The car should maintain good directional stability and the brakes should not fade. When brakes fade, they require substantially more pedal pressure to produce the same braking result.

Wheel alignment

To check the wheel alignment, select a level section of road with light traffic. At normal driving speeds the car should track straight ahead with your hands off the wheel. To compensate for crosswinds,

Test the car under all conditions including full acceleration and panic braking.

make the same test going in the opposite direction. If the car continues to pull to one side, the alignment is off.

Aligning the wheels is not a serious proposition. But if the car isn't tracking true it could have a bent frame or damaged suspension. To quickly check whether the rear wheels are properly following the front wheels, stand directly behind the car and have the seller drive it away from you. If the car seems to be doing a crab imitation, scratch it off your list.

Steering and suspension

The steering should be positive and predictable. Any sign of wandering, looseness or unusual handling characteristics means front end or suspension repairs are needed. A shimmy or shaking and vibrating of the steering wheel at certain speeds only is an indication that the wheels are out of balance. This is not usually an expensive condition to correct.

Drive over a section of bumpy road. A used car won't be as rattle free as a new one. But you shouldn't hear any loud thumping or banging sounds. If the car bounces excessively or slams over the bumps, the suspension and/or shock absorbers need attention or replacement. Steering should remain even and positive over rough roads with a minimum of road shocks transmitted through the wheel.

Make several sharp turns at low speed, and then at a slightly higher speed. The steering should remain smooth with no hesitation or binding, and the car should not pitch or sway excessively.

Noises

Every moving part in a car wears to varying degrees. And worn or damaged parts usually make noise. Drive at normal speeds in an underpass or near parked cars. A solid surface such as a wall tends to reflect sound and makes it easier to hear any noises that the car is making.

Be sure to have the windows open. A steady humming or whining sound that changes in pitch with the car speed could well be a rear end on its way to lunch. A steady scraping sound could indicate dragging brakes, defective wheel bearings or even pebbles in the hubcap. Make a note of any sounds you hear for further investigation with a mechanic. Naturally, the louder the sound, the more you should be concerned. One exception is the high pitched squeal of a slipping fan belt. This is easily corrected with a simple adjustment or a new belt.

When listening to sounds, try to notice if they vary with the speed of the engine or the speed of the car. Running the car in different gears or letting it coast in neutral for a short distance can help to diagnose the source of a hard to identify noise.

Smells

Just as cars are designed to operate silently, so are they made to be relatively odor free. Fumy odors can be caused by a faulty exhaust system or oil leaking onto a hot surface. Burnt smells can mean a dragging brake, an electrical problem or an overheated component. Odors are not only uncomfortable, they can also be dangerous. They indicate that expensive repairs are most likely needed.

The second once over

When you've completed the road test, check over the engine and under the car for signs of leaks. Recheck the engine oil. If you see evidence of water or if the oil level on the dipstick is higher than it was initially, suspect a damaged engine that is allowing coolant to mix with the oil—grounds for immediate disqualification. Another way to check for this is to allow a couple of drops of oil to fall from the dipstick onto a hot exhaust manifold. The oil should smoke but not sizzle. If it does sizzle, this indicates that water is mixed with the oil. In addition, the oil shouldn't smell of gasoline, which could mean worn piston rings. Let the car sit a while with the engine off, and then make a final inspection for any leaks.

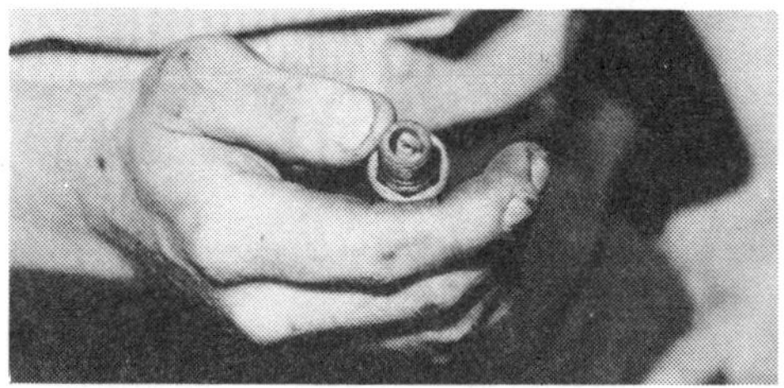

Spark plugs can tell an experienced mechanic a lot about an engine's condition.

The double check

If the car passes your own evaluation, safeguard your investment by bringing it to your own mechanic. Do not use the dealer's mechanic. Bring your list of questions and notes. In addition to checking out your observations, the mechanic should perform additional inspections. With the car up on a lift, he can check the condition of the exhaust system and notice evidence of previous frame damage. He can pull a wheel and check the bearings, disc caliper and rotors, brake linings, drums and wheel cylinders. Suspension problems like leaking shock absorbers are more apparent from under the car. Likewise, the status of the ball joints and front end components can be more critically evaluated. He'll be able to

The mechanic has special tools to determine if the engine is operating correctly.

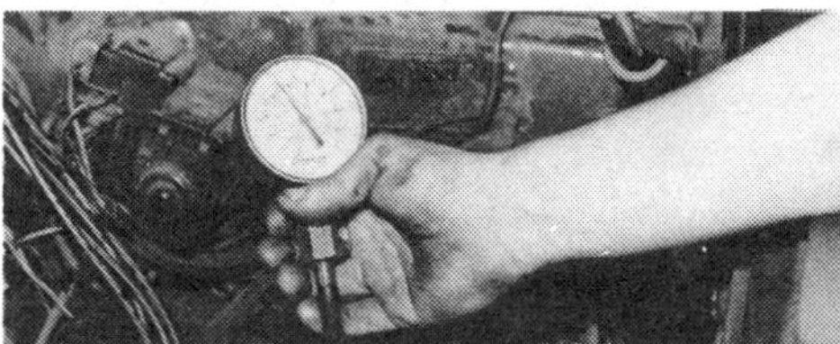

A compression gauge fits into the spark plug holes and reveals engine maladies.

Pulling a wheel is a sure way to determine condition of brake drums and linings.

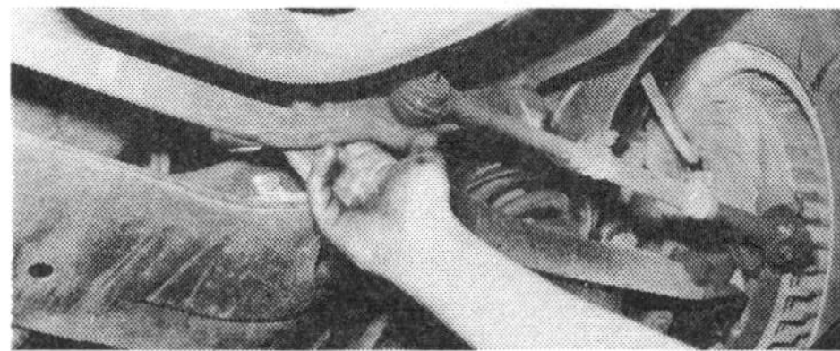

With the car up on the lift, the mechanic can check steering components for wear.

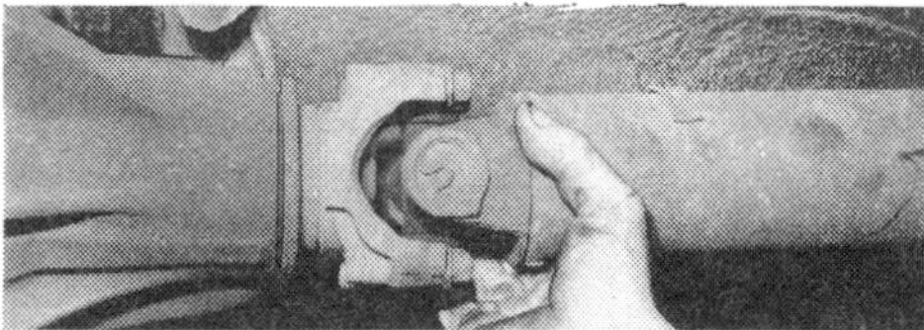

Worn universal joints can be a source of annoying clunks when shifting gears.

spot rust and rot problems that were not obvious on the dealer's lot. And he'll be able to report more authoritatively on the seriousness of any leaks.

Using special instruments, he can better determine the condition of your engine by testing its compression and vacuum. An experienced mechanic can tell a lot about an engine just by looking at its spark plugs. You should also get an estimate of how much money is necessary to correct any problems including things like worn fan belts or hoses and replacing the air filter.

Except for major defects which are grounds for immediate rejection, you'll have to weigh the cost of any repairs along with the final asking price of the car.

High performance cars

Supercars. Muscle cars. Performance cars. Call them what you will. They're a special breed of car no longer being built. But they still offer the driving excitement that is missing from current models. They were produced from the mid '60s to around 1970 and require their own special considerations.

Problems relating to these cars are modifications made for additional performance and hard use. These cars require premium octane fuel and sometimes have such high compression ratios that the highest pump octane available today will not prevent the engines from pinging. In addition to their need for premium fuel, these large performance engines consume gasoline like a tornado consumes houses.

There are also other problems to consider. Some super performance engines were produced in limited quantity which leads to a parts problem. The car may have been modified for dragstrip duty and have extreme rear axle ratios and suspensions that are undesirable for street use.

These cars should be extra carefully checked for signs of severe use. Wheel bearings that contain light oil instead of heavy grease shows this friction cutting trick was used to improve dragstrip times. In standard transmission cars, cracks in the boss where the forks go into the case are a sign of hard shifting. Check for twisted splines on the driveshaft or in the

High performance cars most likely have seen hard use and might have been raced.

transmission by breaking the driveline at a U-joint and pushing the joint towards the transmission. If the splines are straight, the joint will move right in. Twisted splines are a sign of very severe use.

Look for evidence that high performance accessories like traction bars were removed. Another indication that the car was used for racing is the installation of a scattershield around the clutch components.

A high performance car may sound like fun, but they often turn out to be as much fun as a parking ticket. Also expect your insurance company to celebrate the good news of your new muscle car by raising your rates.

Convertibles

A dying breed due to federal safety regulations, the ragtops can appear to be as much fun as the high performance car. Pay special attention to the motor and mechanism that operates the top.

Sports cars

The same cautions apply as to high performance cars. Sports cars usually are driven hard, so pay special attention to the entire drivetrain. Many models are convertibles and are notorious for their lack of weather protection. Check the interior for signs of water leaks.

Some cars may have been used for competition which may leave them with a limited useful life span. Check for racing parts which may not have been removed and evidence of high performance parts which were removed.

Check tires for unusual wear. Suspensions that have been adjusted and tuned for the track are unsuitable for street use. Some imported models are noted for using inferior rubber components. Check fan belts and other rubber parts for signs of deterioration. Check wiring systems for makeshift repairs and evidence of decay.

The next step

If you've found a car that checks out and you've satisfied yourself that it will suit your driving needs, you're ready to do some head to head negotiating.

Mechanic Or Diagnostic Checkout

Be sure to have all these items checked by a professional mechanic or diagnostician before making a final deal on any car.

Engine

1. Compression
2. Vacuum
3. Spark plug reading
4. Noises
5. Leaks
6. Oil condition
7. Carburetion
8. Fuel pump
9. Ignition
10. Exhaust system

Electrical System

1. Alternator
2. Regulator
3. Battery
4. Wiring
5. Air conditioner

Brakes

1. Lining/pads
2. Drums/rotors
3. Hydraulic systems.

Driveline

1. Transmission
2. Universal joints
3. Rear end

Suspension and Front End

1. Shocks
2. Springs
3. Ball joints
4. Steering
5. Alignment
6. Wheel balance

Frame and Body

1. Evidence of structural damage/repair
2. Rust
3. Gas tank damage

Car Condition Check List

EXTERIOR

ITEM	LOOK FOR	PROBLEM?
Paint	New paint on late model, mismatches in color.	yes☐ no☐
Body	Ripples (evidence of body work).	yes☐ no☐
	Rust or rot.	yes☐ no☐
Chrome	New or unmatched bumpers, trim, grille, doorhandles.	yes☐ no☐
Body/frame	Misaligned doors, hood or trunk lid. Doors sag when open, evidence of frame repair.	yes☐ no☐
Suspension	Sags.	yes☐ no☐
Exhaust system	Rust, holes, gunk in tailpipe.	yes☐ no☐
Tires	Poor condition, uneven tread wear, new retreads.	yes☐ no☐
Front end	Play or noise when shaking front wheels.	yes☐ no☐
Trunk	Rust, evidence of hard use, check spare tire.	yes☐ no☐

INTERIOR

ITEM	LOOK FOR	PROBLEM?
Evidence of detailing	Paint overspray, new seatcovers, new headliner, condition doesn't jibe with mileage.	yes☐ no☐
Upholstery	Sagging, worn, seat adjustment does not operate freely.	yes☐ no☐
Driver's door handle	Loose or sloppy.	yes☐ no☐
Armrests	Worn or frayed.	yes☐ no☐
Foot pedals	Operate freely without excessive play.	yes☐ no☐
Foot pedal pads	Condition jibes with mileage, excessively worn or brand new.	yes☐ no☐
Floor mats	Reasonable wear.	yes☐ no☐

INTERIOR (continued)

ITEM	LOOK FOR	PROBLEM?
Door locks	Operate positively.	yes ☐ no ☐
Parking brake	No binding.	yes ☐ no ☐
Windshield wiper	Operative.	yes ☐ no ☐
Instruments	Complete and operative.	yes ☐ no ☐
Radio	Operative.	yes ☐ no ☐
Heater and air conditioner	Adequate temperature output.	yes ☐ no ☐
Other options or accessories	Operable.	yes ☐ no ☐
Driver's side window and vent window	No binding or looseness.	yes ☐ no ☐
All other windows	Operate freely, evidence of leaks.	yes ☐ no ☐
Ignition switch	Excessive key wear.	yes ☐ no ☐
Other locks	Work smoothly, evidence of replacement.	yes ☐ no ☐
Weatherstripping	Worn or loose fitting.	yes ☐ no ☐
Steering wheel rim	Worn.	yes ☐ no ☐
All lights	Headlights—both beams, brake, tail, parking, back up and license plate lights, turn signals, emergency flasher operable.	yes ☐ no ☐
Horn	Operable.	yes ☐ no ☐
Windshield	Damaged or scratched, evidence of leaks.	yes ☐ no ☐
Rear window	Damaged or scratched, evidence of leaks.	yes ☐ no ☐

MECHANICAL

ITEM	LOOK FOR	PROBLEM?
Brake pedal	Firm.	yes ☐ no ☐
Steering wheel	Excessive play, binding.	yes ☐ no ☐
Engine oil	Very heavy, dirty or grayish color.	yes ☐ no ☐

(continued)

MECHANICAL (continued)

ITEM	LOOK FOR	PROBLEM?
Auto transmission oil	Discolored or burnt smell.	yes☐ no☐
Radiator	Dirty, gunk inside filler neck, leaking, evidence of boil over.	yes☐ no☐
Wiring	Frayed.	yes☐ no☐
Seals	Leaks on or around engine or under car.	yes☐ no☐
Dashboard engine warning lights	Operable, go out when engine starts.	yes☐ no☐
Engine start	Sluggish.	yes☐ no☐
Idle speed	Too fast when warmed up, uneven.	yes☐ no☐
Engine noise	Hissing, knocking, ticking, other.	yes☐ no☐
Engine running	Uneven pulse at tailpipe, sluggish response to accelerator pressure.	yes☐ no☐
Exhaust smoke	Black or blue.	yes☐ no☐
Steering	Groans, clunks, binding when turned lock to lock.	yes☐ no☐
Engine/transmission	Leaks when engine is running.	yes☐ no☐
Fluids	Level and condition of engine oil, auto transmission fluid, power steering fluid, brake fluid, battery water (with engine hot).	yes☐ no☐
Hot engine start	Fast starts on five consecutive tries.	yes☐ no☐
Auto transmission	Clunks, jerks, groans or other noises when shifting through the gears. Same symptoms when shifting back and forth between Drive and Reverse.	yes☐ no☐
Shock absorbers	More than one rebound cycle when each corner of car is pushed down.	yes☐ no☐

ROAD TEST— ENGINE/TRANSMISSION

ITEM	LOOK FOR	PROBLEM?
Exhaust smoke	Black or blue.	yes☐ no☐

ENGINE/TRANSMISSION (continued)

ITEM	LOOK FOR	PROBLEM?
Engine	Uneven delivery of power, missing, sluggish, ping, knocks, hot rod sounds or other noises.	yes ☐ no ☐
Auto transmission	Slips, engine racing between shifts, uneven spacing of shifting, poor kickdown gear engagement, noises, whines, other.	yes ☐ no ☐
Standard transmission	Hard shifting, sloppiness in shift linkage, gear or other noises.	yes ☐ no ☐
Clutch	Slips, noises, excessive play or hard operation.	yes ☐ no ☐

BRAKES

ITEM	LOOK FOR	PROBLEM?
Parking brake	Doesn't hold on hill or in gear against light accelerator pressure.	yes ☐ no ☐
Low speed brake test	Wheels lock up evenly, low pedal, soft or spongy pedal feel.	yes ☐ no ☐
High speed brake test	Car doesn't maintain directional stability, fade after three stops, spongy pedal feel.	yes ☐ no ☐

ALIGNMENT

ITEM	LOOK FOR	PROBLEM?
Wheel and frame alignment	Car pulls to one side on straight and level road. Appears to travel crabwise when viewed from the rear.	yes ☐ no ☐

STEERING/SUSPENSION

ITEM	LOOK FOR	PROBLEM?
Steering	Loose, wandering, binding, noises, clunks, wheel vibration, shimmy or road shocks transmitted through steering wheel.	yes ☐ no ☐
Suspension	Bouncy ride, excessive sway, poor directional control, hard ride or banging.	yes ☐ no ☐

(continued)

GENERAL

ITEM	LOOK FOR	PROBLEM?
Noises	Whine, hum, knocks, rattling, scraping—determine whether steady and if it varies with the speed of the car or the speed of the engine.	yes☐ no☐
Odors	Fumy, burning, gasoline, other	yes☐ no☐
Leak recheck	Leaks around engine or under car	yes☐ no☐

Evaluation

Now that you have a list of things to look for and potential problems, you might judge whether to reject the car on the spot or invest in the services of a mechanic or diagnostic center. Serious defects like evidence of frame damage or an oil burning engine are grounds for immediate rejection.

The big problem is translating symptoms such as engine noises into dollar and cents repairs. If you're mechanically knowledgeable, you can differentiate between the sounds of a stuck valve lifter and a worn piston pin, or a transmission that requires a $12 band adjustment or a $300 overhaul.

Obviously, the more things wrong with a car, the more money you'll have to put into it to correct the problems. But here again you have to weigh the variables of not correcting minor problems, doing the work yourself and the price of the car. If you have a choice between two very similar cars, you might think that all you have to do is select the car with fewer problems or the lower estimated repair bill. Take the case of two cars with equal mileage. One appears to have been driven harder, but has relatively few defects at present. The other car seems to have had an easier life but requires $75 more in repair bills. Your selection should take into account how long you intend keeping the car and the chances of future problems.

Estimate Your Necessary Repairs

	Estimated cost		Estimated cost
Engine	$ ______	**Paint**	$ ______
Cooling system	______	**Glass**	______
Exhaust	______	**Interior**	______
Transmission	______	**Tires**	______
Differential	______	**Electrical**	______
Suspension	______	**Accessories**	______
Steering	______	**Miscellaneous**	______
Bodywork	______		

Wheeling And Dealing

The salesman has the advantage in haggling over a car because of his experience.

Buying a car, new or used, is different from buying almost anything else in our society. When you shop for a suit of clothes, a TV or groceries, you check price tags and buy where they are lowest. "Eighty-five dollars for that dishwasher? Who do I make the check payable to?" Not so when buying a car.

Perhaps because the automobile directly superseded the horse did the concept of horse trading or bargaining become an established way of doing business. If you consider haggling over price a difficult experience, imagine what it's like in some other countries where you have to bargain over the price of everything you buy.

What you're up against

Because haggling is synonymous with the car business, some dealers employ salesmen who are specialists in handling specific areas of the transaction, similar to the situation existing in the medical profession. These specialists even have unique titles. First there's the Liner. He's the first salesman you meet—the official greeter. He's a cheerful one-of-the-boys type whose job it is to put you at ease and in a receptive mood. He then very skillfully turns you over to a regular salesman who recommends suitable cars, arranges test rides and gives you the general sales pitch. When you're sold on a car he turns you over to the Closer. These changes can be made so smoothly that you never get the feeling that you're being shuttled from salesman to salesman. The Closer is an expert at making deals. He's the dollars and cents man. The shrewdest buyer is a rank amateur compared to an experienced Closer. He can skin the cat five different ways, juggling figures on trade-in, financing and insurance so skillfully that the average buyer doesn't realize how much he's actually paying for his car.

Smaller dealers don't have this variety of sales talent, but they have developed their own techniques for moving cars off their lots. No matter how low pressure or friendly a dealer appears, don't lose sight of the fact that he's there to sell cars, and at the best possible price—for him.

Haggling

The normal course of events begins with the salesman quoting you a price. This is a gesture akin to boxers shaking hands in the ring before the bout and is not to be taken seriously. If you agree to this initial price, the salesman will be shocked and may have a heart attack. Even if you say nothing at all and look at him with a blank stare, he will come down in price.

In any bargaining either with a dealer or private party quote a price that's 25% less than you're prepared to pay. That way, you will have room to come up in price while the seller is coming down.

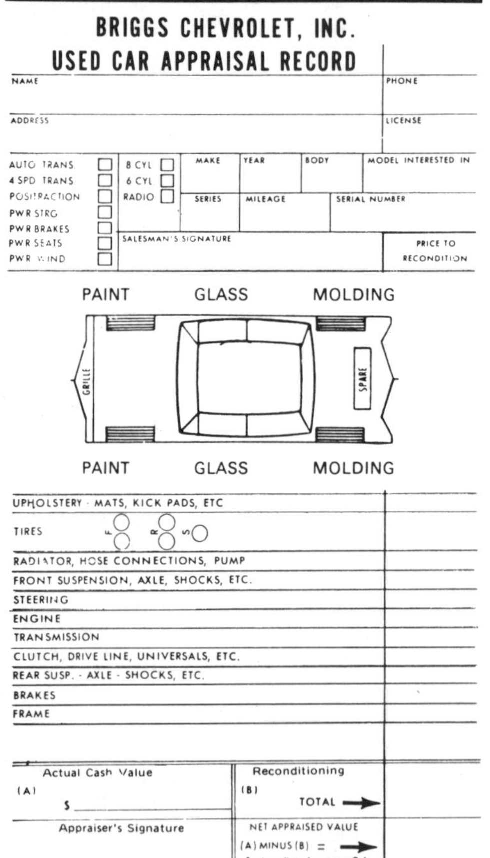

BRIGGS CHEVROLET, INC.
USED CAR APPRAISAL RECORD

NAME | PHONE
ADDRESS | LICENSE

AUTO TRANS. ☐
4 SPD TRANS ☐
POSITRACTION ☐
PWR STRG ☐
PWR BRAKES ☐
PWR SEATS ☐
PWR WIND ☐
8 CYL ☐
6 CYL ☐
RADIO ☐

MAKE | YEAR | BODY | MODEL INTERESTED IN
SERIES | MILEAGE | SERIAL NUMBER
SALESMAN'S SIGNATURE | PRICE TO RECONDITION

UPHOLSTERY - MATS, KICK PADS, ETC
TIRES F R S
RADIATOR, HOSE CONNECTIONS, PUMP
FRONT SUSPENSION, AXLE, SHOCKS, ETC.
STEERING
ENGINE
TRANSMISSION
CLUTCH, DRIVE LINE, UNIVERSALS, ETC.
REAR SUSP. - AXLE - SHOCKS, ETC.
BRAKES
FRAME

Actual Cash Value (A) $ ______ | Reconditioning (B) TOTAL →
Appraiser's Signature | NET APPRAISED VALUE (A) MINUS (B) = → For Immediate Acceptance Only

Some dealers use their own check-out list to appraise your trade-in.

There are exceptions to this rigmarole. A car dealer, like any other businessman, will occasionally run a bonafide sale. He will advertise cars at, or very close to, their wholesale price just to build traffic on his lot. He will advertise the serial numbers and any special equipment on the cars. This is one of the few times you can get a car for a rock bottom price on a straightforward deal.

Be alert to deals which look like bargains on the surface but actually are not. In this instance, the dealer advertises cars at unbeatable prices. He also will give you a generous trade-in allowance for your car. How does he make money? On the financing end of the deal. His secret is to spread a very high interest rate over a long string of payments (36-48) so it's not obvious. The buyer believes he's ended up with a much sweeter deal than he actually has.

Variables such as trade-in allowances make negotiating more complicated and it is easier to lose sight of the actual cash amount you will be paying for a car. One common dealer practice is to offer you a higher trade-in allowance for your car. But the salesman will quote you a higher price initially for the car in which you've expressed an interest. This fools some buyers into thinking they're getting a better deal than if a lower trade-in offer were made with a correspondingly lower price quote on the dealer's car. Always keep in mind the actual cash difference between the dealer's offer for your car and the price for his. Never get sidetracked with tempting gambits like "The car will cost you only x dollars a month." You don't know at this point how many months you'll be paying or what kind of interest charges you're being hit with. Keep the negotiations simple. If you intend financing the car, first settle on a final price and then take up the matter of payments.

Each salesman has his own sales technique that works for him. One method used to get a buyer into direct negotiation is "low balling" or offering him a low price for his trade-in. This can be an effective shock treatment and the buyer immediately is on the defensive saying his car is worth much more than the offer. The salesman reconsiders and modifies his offer and the buyer feels like he's making headway and is drawn into the bargaining, which is what the salesman wanted all along.

If a satisfactory price isn't arrived at and you start to leave to see if you can do better elsewhere, you will probably be thrown the "highball." The salesman tells you he thinks he can talk his manager into coming up with more money on a trade-in and maybe reducing the price of the car x dollars at the same time. This last offer usually will be very attractive—so much so that the competition will be unable to beat it. If you return to the dealer, the salesman will invariably tell you that his manager didn't go for his deal. But he has accomplished his purpose. You're back on his lot. And he most likely will come up with a slightly better proposition than his last firm offer.

Remember, nothing is final until it is on paper.

Another trick a salesman might pull is to show you the wholesale price in the guidebook on the car you want. He'll say something like, "Look, I'm only making $25 over what the car cost me." He may conveniently forget to mention that the book price is for a car in first-class condition, or that he bought the car at auction at well below the current wholesale price.

If you feel that you're not getting the rock bottom price on a car, and you aren't under pressure to buy, simply say goodbye and leave. Return the following week and see if the car is still available. If it is, the dealer will probably come down in his price. If the car doesn't sell, he will have to wholesale it and wind up with less profit than if he dropped his retail price.

Having the facts puts you in the best bargaining position. Sometimes a customer puts one over on the dealer by cleverly disguising a serious defect on a car he trades in. Not all dealers go over the trade-ins as carefully as they should and consequently may tag the car with a higher price than its worth. The time to bring up all the imperfections you found in your thorough inspection is when you're talking dollars and cents with the dealer. Try for the lowest price you can and then bring up the defects you found for an even lower reduction in price. Don't expect the dealer to deduct the retail cost of repairs as he can do them on a wholesale level. But expect some price adjustment, or dealer repairs. Otherwise, back off from negotiations.

After the salesman points out the car's desirable features, bring up its defects.

Getting extras thrown in

Dealers will sometimes throw in extras, or accessories, instead of coming down in price. Consider if you would really benefit by these accessories, as the dealer is paying wholesale or less for these items and is using them with retail leverage. In many instances, you can add options to your car later at discount prices by shopping the discount auto accessory stores.

You can bring up the subject of extras or accessories during haggling or right before final price agreement. Use lines like: "Twelve-fifty is a steep price for a car with only an AM radio." With this gambit, you're bouncing the ball back in the salesman's court with the hint that you might be more receptive to his offer if the pot were sweetened with an AM-FM radio or possibly a tape deck.

If the salesman finally meets your figure, try for a bonus with something like: "Fourteen hundred. I don't know. Tell you what. Throw in two new front tires to replace those retreads, and you've got a deal."

Sometimes, even after a deal is made, you can reel in extras by capitalizing on the dealer's good will. "Fourteen hundred? It's a deal. But you don't want me to drive out of here with those ragged looking floor mats do you?" or "I'd sure feel a lot more secure if I had a better spare tire."

Other extras you should try for are undercoating to better protect the underbody of your car from road salt, rust and corrosion, seat covers, or even a thorough tuneup.

The experienced haggler never gets excited or insulting. You can accomplish much more by being pleasant and agreeable. Don't say, "That car is a piece of junk and not worth a penny over $900." Try a different tack: "The car looks like it's worth the money. Trouble is, I'm on this strict budget and anything over $900 would really be pushing it. Then I have to figure on spending money to fix the fram-its which I notice doesn't work."

Be positive, but not overly enthusiastic. If you see the car of your dreams, be cool. If the salesman sees you slobbering all over a car, he'll figure you'll pull one of the kids out of college to meet the payments—and bargain accordingly.

Used car warranties

A used car warranty is only as good as the dealer you buy your car from. The practical value of these warranties is vastly overestimated by car buyers. It's a fact that any dealer can fail to live up to a warranty if he wants to, or fool the buyer into thinking he is living up to the terms of the agreement, when in truth he is not.

Some dealers will say that a low mileage late-model car is still covered by the original manufacturer's warranty. Most car makers do not allow the warranty to pass to subsequent car owners without their specific permission and sometimes the payment of a fee. Check with the manufacturer's local District Service Manager if you have any doubts.

Any used car warranty must be put in writing. If the fine print on the contract says the warranty must be spelled out on a separate sheet of paper, then warranty

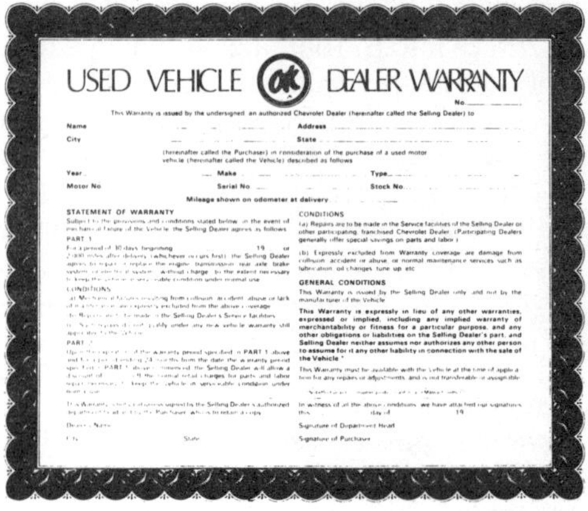

USED VEHICLE OK DEALER WARRANTY

No. ______

This Warranty is issued by the undersigned an authorized Chevrolet Dealer (hereinafter called the Selling Dealer) to

Name ______ Address ______

City ______ State ______

(hereinafter called the Purchaser) in consideration of the purchase of a used motor vehicle (hereinafter called the Vehicle) described as follows

Year ______ Make ______ Type ______

Motor No ______ Serial No ______ Stock No ______

Mileage shown on odometer at delivery ______

STATEMENT OF WARRANTY

Subject to the provisions and conditions stated below in the event of mechanical failure of the Vehicle the Selling Dealer agrees as follows

PART 1

For a period of 30 days beginning ______ 19 ___ or 2,000 miles after delivery (whichever occurs first) the Selling Dealer agrees to repair or replace the engine transmission rear axle brake system or electrical system without charge to the extent necessary to keep the vehicle in serviceable condition under normal use

CONDITIONS

(a) Mechanical failures resulting from collision accident abuse or lack of maintenance are expressly excluded from the above coverage

(b) Repairs are to be made in the Selling Dealer's Service facilities

PART 2

Upon the expiration of the warranty period specified in PART 1 above ... the Selling Dealer will allow a discount of ... of the normal retail charges for parts and labor

CONDITIONS

(a) Repairs are to be made in the Service facilities of the Selling Dealer or other participating franchised Chevrolet Dealer. (Participating Dealers generally offer special savings on parts and labor.)

(b) Expressly excluded from Warranty coverage are damage from collision accident or abuse, or normal maintenance services such as lubrication oil changes tune up etc

GENERAL CONDITIONS

This Warranty is issued by the Selling Dealer only and not by the manufacturer of the Vehicle

This Warranty is expressly in lieu of any other warranties, expressed or implied, including any implied warranty of merchantability or fitness for a particular purpose, and any other obligations or liabilities on the Selling Dealer's part, and Selling Dealer neither assumes nor authorizes any other person to assume for it any other liability in connection with the sale of the Vehicle."

This Warranty must be available with the Vehicle at the time of application for any repairs or adjustments, and is not transferable or assignable

In witness of all the above conditions we have attached our signatures this ______ day of ______ 19 ___

Dealer Name ______ Signature of Department Head ______

City ______ State ______ Signature of Purchaser ______

No guarantee is valid unless it's in writing.

terms penciled in on the sales contract are legally worthless.

Used car warranties come in all shapes and sizes. Some dealers may offer you just a 15% discount on parts for a limited period of time. Don't get too excited about this type of warranty, as you can probably get the same, if not better, discount at your local discount auto parts outlet. And the dealer certainly will profit on his labor charges.

Some dealers offer an extended warranty on their cars through outside sources.

The usual used car warranty is the 50-50. Under this agreement, you and the dealer split the cost of any repairs that are required during the first 30 days or 1000 miles. Sounds fair enough on the surface. But the dealer comes out ahead. Way ahead. To begin with, he gets his parts at wholesale prices and pays his mechanics 50% of the labor rate. He charges you the

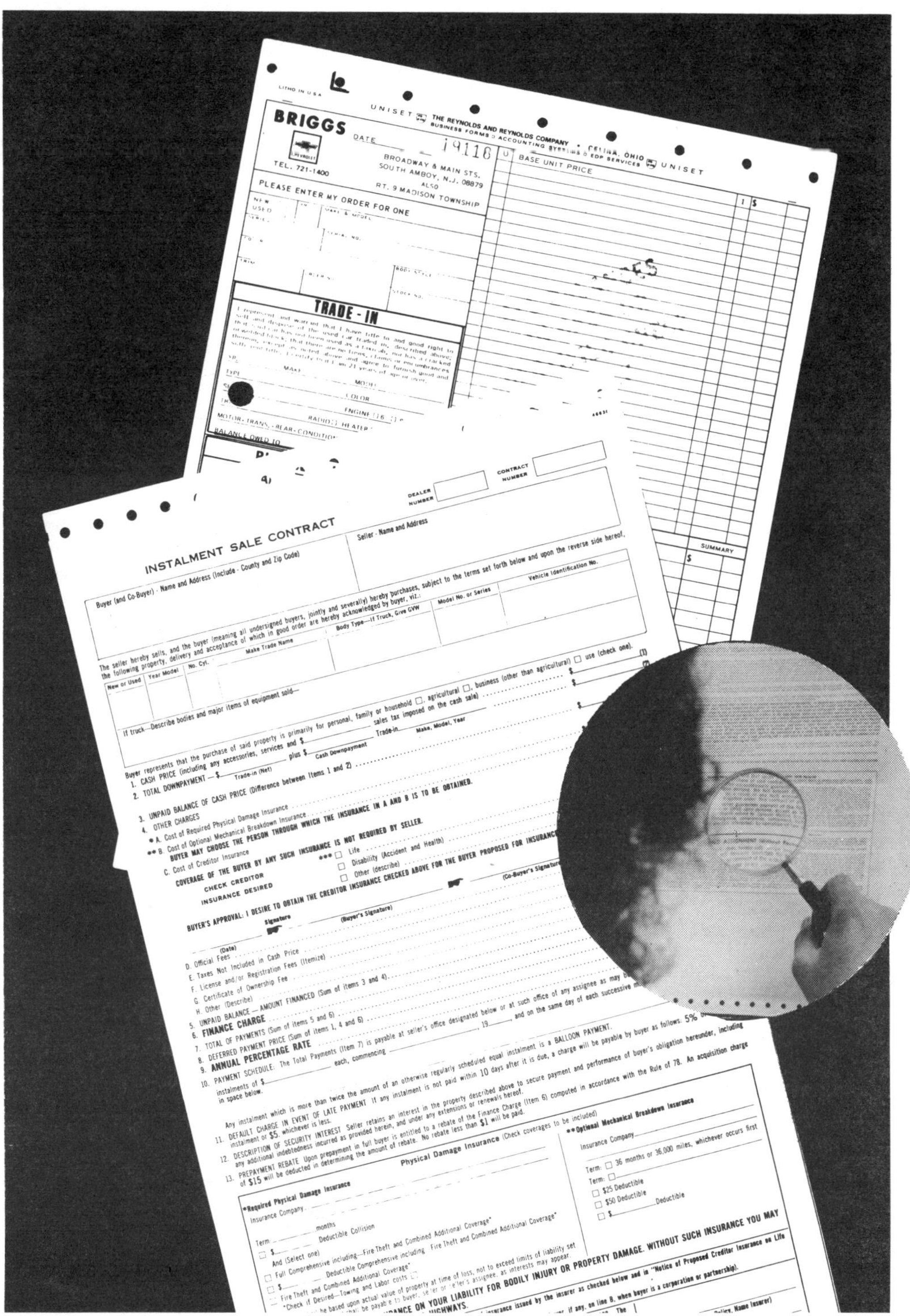

Sales contracts are complicated and binding. Understand what you are signing. Read the fine print carefully on all documents. If you have questions, seek advice.

regular retail price for parts and labor. Some dealers even go beyond this and farm your car out for repair at another service outlet. The dealer gives you a bill for twice what the repairs cost him and not a nickel leaves his pocket.

Then there's the 100% unconditional guarantee. How can you go wrong? Take a magnifying glass and read the fine print. You'll discover that the guarantee is anything but unconditional. There are exclusions galore, like tires and glass. Those items are understandable, but how about terms like software, which is open to dealer interpretation and can mean anything from upholstery to wiring. The warranty might also limit coverage on items relating to wheel alignment. Interpret that to mean the dealer can bow out of any and all front end repairs including replacing defective ball joints.

If this isn't enough to disillusion you, the rest of the fine print will. Some 100% warranties state that in order to keep the warranty in effect, you have to maintain a very stringent service schedule, use specific brands of products and specified service outlets.

How about a money back guarantee? You certainly can't beat that. Don't underestimate the used car dealer. The gimmick with this sort of guarantee is that you have to return the car within 24 hours and pay a service charge anywhere up to $50. You're better off renting a new car for that kind of money.

Another come on is the trial exchange warranty. You're not happy with the car you bought? Come back and pick out another one of equal value and the dealer will exchange, even up. Let's say your car had a sticker price of $1595, but you were able to get $300 knocked off the price. The only cars you'll be able to swap for will be limited to the ones with a maximum sticker price of $1295. Or if prices aren't marked, which is a growing trend these days, the salesman will conveniently jack up the asking price accordingly of any car you select. Only this time, you're in no position to bargain.

Quick Facts: How To Wheel And Deal

- Make your first offer 25% less than you're prepared to pay.
- Never lose sight of the actual total dollar amount you will pay. Don't be sidetracked by seemingly generous trade-in offers or low monthly payments.
- Arrange for financing and credit approval in advance.
- Don't put much faith in a salesman's statements concerning a car's history or how little profit the dealer is making on the sale.
- Never get excited or angry during negotiations.
- If you can't get the car at your price, check back with the dealer the following week.
- Bring up any defects or flaws that you've found in the car during hard price bargaining, not before.
- Consider desirable extras or options that the dealer will include in lieu of a price reduction. But be alert to those items that you can obtain inexpensively on your own through discount auto parts and accessory outlets.
- Push for extras just before reaching a final price.
- Learn in advance if any deposits are refundable.
- Make sure any agreements or understandings are specifically written into the sales contract. Read the contract thoroughly.
- Make sure the dealer or salesman has signed the sales agreement and that there are no figures or information missing.
- Do not leave car with the dealer after it is officially yours.

The ultimate weapon of car dealers when it comes to warranty work is the runaround. You bring your car in for service and it's shuttled to a corner of the service department or car lot. It's returned to you in the same shape that you brought it in. So you have to make another trip to the dealer's service department. And the same thing happens. Sooner or later, you'll get tired and fed up and forget the whole thing.

Reputable dealers, on the other hand, will perform legitimate warranty work, and a few have been known to honor the warranty on some items even after it has expired. These dealers put a tangible value on good will.

Some dealers mark up the price of their cars 10% to cover themselves for warranty work. Sometimes the dealers will come down on the price of the car if you forego the warranty. It can be a lot cheaper to take the latter option and invest some of your savings in a thorough checkout by a qualified mechanic or diagnostic center.

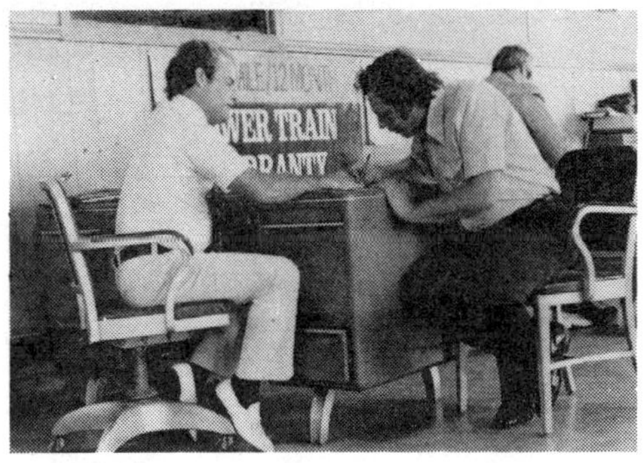

When you feel you've reached a good deal, it's time for the paperwork. Before signing any documents or contracts, make sure all blanks are filled in. Make sure that any verbal agreements are spelled out in writing. Read the entire sales agreement as carefully as you inspected the car. It's important that you understand every item in the contract. Don't lose the advantages you gained in driving a hard bargain because of a failure to read the fine print. Make sure the dealer has signed the contract. Otherwise it is not binding. If you want the agreement explained to you by your lawyer, the dealer should have no objection. Only then should you sign your name on the dotted line. Remember, you're signing a legal document. Know what you're signing.

The fine print

Read the entire sales agreement as carefully as you inspected the car. And make sure you understand every item. Many advantages gained in driving a hard bargain have been lost because of failure to read or fully understand the fine print. A sales contract is a legal document and some wording may be intentionally complex. Play it safe and don't take the salesman's interpretation of the contract. The dealer should have no objection if you want the agreement explained to you by your lawyer.

Any verbal promises made regarding optional equipment, repairs, financial terms, guarantees, etc. are meaningless unless they are written specifically into the agreement.

Do not sign the sales contract unless it is complete. If there are any empty spaces where there should be numbers, insist that they be filled in before you sign. Also make sure that the dealer or salesman has already signed the contract which is not binding unless all parties have signed. There are cases where dealers have changed their mind about a sale, and if they haven't signed the agreement, there is nothing you can do.

Many buyers will put a deposit on a car to hold it while they arrange for financing, disposing of their old car, etc. Keep your deposit as low as possible, as opposed to a down payment which should be as high as possible, so if you decide to call the deal off, you will not be out too much money if the fine print says your deposit is not refundable.

One thing to be especially alert to is that most sales contracts state that the dealer has the right to reappraise your trade-in at the time of sale. There can be a considerable difference between his original offer for your car and the final figure.

Once the agreement is signed and the car officially sold, do not leave it on the dealer's premises. Some unscrupulous dealers have been known to remove items such as tape decks and claim they were never on the car. If these items were not listed in the sales agreement, there is little you can do.

Financing Your Used Car

Some bank loans can be obtained at low rates using savings or stocks as security.

Few people have the means to buy a car and plunk down cash for the full purchase price. Hence, the great American institution of buying on time.

Financing a car can be as simple as an agreement between a private buyer and seller to split the purchase price into two or more installments, or become so complex when involving commercial contracts that the buyer gets lost somewhere between the first dollar sign and the final period.

Where to get money

Money for financing your car is available from several sources. How much you end up paying for a loan will depend on factors such as your credit rating—if you have a history of paying bills or installments on time, your rating will be good—how much you borrow, how long you take to pay back and where you borrow from. The greater risk you appear to be to the lender, the higher the cost of the loan. You obtain the best rates when the lender has the most assurance that you will repay the loan.

Passbook loans offer the lowest rates. You offer the bank your savings account as collateral against the loan. Your account has to contain more money than you are borrowing. With this type of loan, you are not allowed to touch the money in your account until the loan is repaid. If you happen to need money to cover an emergency during this period, you must borrow as if your savings account didn't exist. Why not just withdraw the money from your account in the first place? Many people feel that without the pressure of regular monthly payments that have to be met, they would be less than diligent about repaying a loan to themselves.

Another type of low interest loan is borrowing against stocks. Most banks will loan you up to 75% of the value of your stocks which they hold as security. The bank's investment department usually determines the fair value of the stocks. As with a passbook loan, the stocks are in the bank's control until the loan is repaid. This loan isn't as straightforward as the passbook loan as it depends on which stocks you own and the current and projected state of the stock market.

Borrowing on life insurance policies if they're the kind that have a cash redemption value (whole life policies) can net you money at some of the most favorable rates. The disadvantage is that, on some policies while the loan is still outstanding, your beneficiary would collect only a fraction of the policy's face amount if something happened to you. So you have to weigh the low interest rates against possible reduced protection for your family. Some auto insurance companies also make loans, although interest rates fluctuate widely. Work through your independent agent to check out these loans. He'll try to get you the best rate he can because he has an interest in keeping your insurance business.

Credit unions, whether connected with your employment union or public, are a very good source of cash as they have very reasonable interest rates and require a relatively small amount of collateral. One big advantage in dealing through a credit union is that you're not penalized as severely as by other lending institutions should you desire to pay off your loan early. Paying off a 12-month bank loan in six months would save you not 50% of the interest as you would expect, but only a little more than 25% in most cases.

Bank loans usually have higher interest charges than all of the preceding sources for money we've discussed. Interest rates will vary between banks so it pays to shop around. Large banks often offer better rates than smaller ones, but your own credit standing also is a telling factor.

Finance companies have some of the highest interest rates. This is because, generally speaking, they are willing to accept poorer credit risks than the banks. Turn to the finance companies only if you have exhausted the possibilities of doing business with the other lending institutions. The finance company may require more collateral than the car. This is because some lenders who foresee repayment difficulties will neglect maintaining the car because it will be repossessed anyway. The value of a neglected car could drop well below the amount still owed by the borrower. So the finance company has to hedge their bet. They do this by securing additional collateral like your furniture, jewelry or anything else of tangible value.

If you do secure a loan through a finance company and pay it off on time, your credit rating may improve to the point where you could secure future loans through a bank or other lending institutions.

Banks, under certain circumstances, have made it very easy to obtain loans. Some offer a specific amount of money that is constantly available for your use. This feature may be plugged into your checking account so that by writing a check for more than your balance, you automatically draw on this reserve money, and, in effect, write yourself a loan. You pay interest only on the amount of the loan that's currently outstanding. And you can pay up as soon as you like with no prepayment penalty.

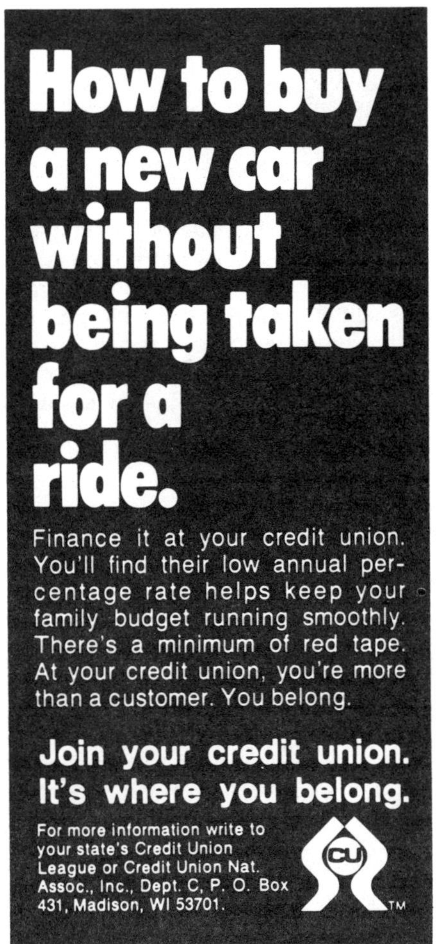

Credit unions, both private and public, are a good source of financing for cars. Interest rates are low.

Similar to this program is the line-of-credit offered by certain credit card operations. A fixed amount of money is always on reserve and available to you either by writing a line-of-credit check, which functions the same way as a personal check, or by receiving instant cash at any of the card's participating bank offices. As you charge purchases with your credit card, or receive cash advances, your maximum amount of credit is reduced accordingly.

One of the most convenient places to obtain financing is the car dealer. Unfortunately, it's usually also the most costly.

Car dealers have several ways of handling finance arrangements. A franchised new car dealer can arrange financing through the manufacturer's credit facility such as General Motors Acceptance Corp. or the Ford Motor Credit Co.

Financing is a source of profit for the dealer and so they push these contracts. A dealer can offer you an installment contract for, say 20% interest and then turn around and sell the contract to a finance company for 15% interest, reaping a quick 5% on the deal. He can obtain preferred rates from a small loan company because he guarantees your payments. If you default, he will repossess the car and resell it.

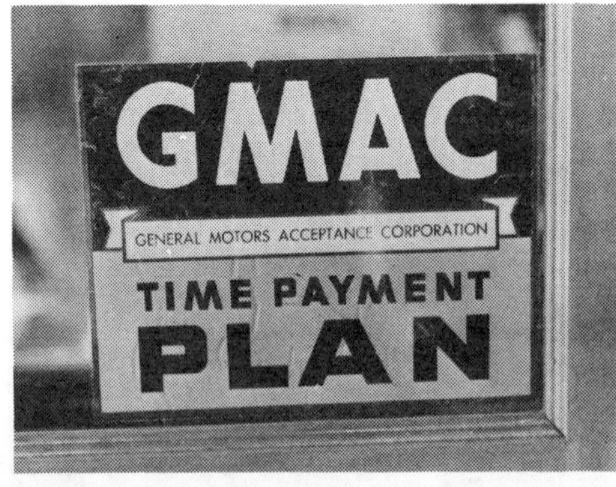

Buying a used car through a franchised new car dealer offers the convenience of one-stop financing through a car manufacturer's credit organization. Interest rates with this method of financing may be higher than those charged by local banks.

Tips on obtaining financing

Shop for financing as carefully as you do your car. Apply first at the lending institutions that offer the lowest interest rates. There is only one way to compare interest rates and that's by obtaining the annual percentage interest rate. The Truth In Lending Law passed in 1969 requires all lending institutions to tell you the annual percentage interest rate. But compliance with this law is not 100%. You may be told that the monthly interest charge is a low 3%. But a quick multiplication by 12 (months) will show you that the annual interest rate on this loan is a not-so-bargain-oriented 36%. The cardinal rule, then, in shopping for financing, is to obtain the annual percentage interest rate.

One way to learn what you are paying in annual interest charges, if the dealer is reluctant to tell you, is to find out what the car would cost if you paid cash. Then deduct this amount from the total cost of the car on installments (amount each month times the number of payments). This is the total dollar amount of interest that you're paying. To figure the annual rate, divide the total dollar amount of interest by the amount of money being financed (the price of the car less down payment and trade-in) and multiply the result by 100.

There are two basic types of loans—those with simple interest and those that are discounted. A simple interest loan charges you interest on your unpaid balance. With each payment your unpaid balance becomes less so your interest gradually decreases over the life of the loan. This type of loan is difficult to obtain. The most common kind of loan involving automobile purchasing is the discount loan. Here, the interest is figured in advance so you're paying interest on the original amount borrowed even though you actually owe less through making payments. The actual interest on discount loans can be deceiving unless you know the annual percentage rate. The dollar amount of interest may be added to the amount you want to borrow or you may actually receive the amount you wish to borrow minus the interest charges. To

No matter what method of financing you finally choose, you will be required to fill out a loan application.

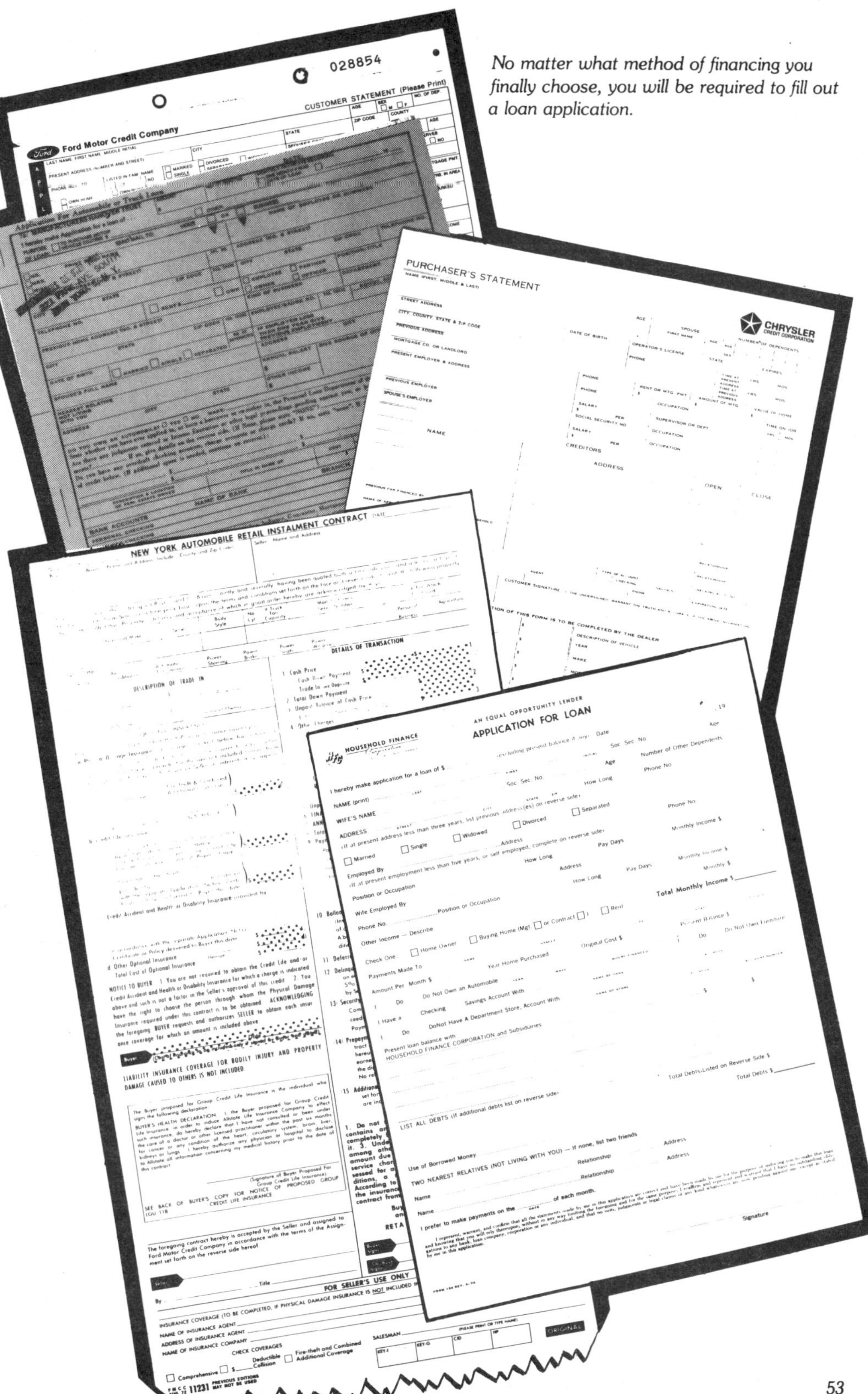

028854

Ford Motor Credit Company

CUSTOMER STATEMENT (Please Print)

PURCHASER'S STATEMENT

CHRYSLER CREDIT CORPORATION

NEW YORK AUTOMOBILE RETAIL INSTALMENT CONTRACT

DETAILS OF TRANSACTION

HOUSEHOLD FINANCE Corporation

AN EQUAL OPPORTUNITY LENDER

APPLICATION FOR LOAN

I hereby make application for a loan of $ ... (excluding present balance if any) Date

NAME (print) Soc. Sec. No. Age Number of Other Dependents

WIFE'S NAME Soc. Sec. No. Age Phone No.

ADDRESS How Long

(If at present address less than three years, list previous address(es) on reverse side)

Married Single Widowed Divorced Separated Phone No.

Employed By Address Pay Days Monthly Income $

(If at present employment less than five years, or self employed, complete on reverse side)

Position or Occupation How Long

Wife Employed By Address Pay Days Monthly Income $

Phone No. Position or Occupation How Long

Other Income — Describe Total Monthly Income $

Check One: Home Owner Buying Home (Mgt or Contract) Rent

Payments Made To Year Home Purchased Original Cost $ Present Balance $

Amount Per Month $ Do Not Own Furniture

I Do Do Not Own an Automobile

I Have a Checking Savings Account With

I Do DoNot Have A Department Store, Account With

Present loan balance with HOUSEHOLD FINANCE CORPORATION and Subsidiaries

Total Debts Listed on Reverse Side $

Total Debts $

LIST ALL DEBTS (If additional debts list on reverse side)

Use of Borrowed Money

TWO NEAREST RELATIVES (NOT LIVING WITH YOU) — If none, list two friends

Name Relationship Address

Name Relationship Address

I prefer to make payments on the ... of each month.

Signature

The foregoing contract hereby is accepted by the Seller and assigned to Ford Motor Credit Company in accordance with the terms of the Assignment set forth on the reverse side hereof.

FOR SELLER'S USE ONLY

INSURANCE COVERAGE (TO BE COMPLETED, IF PHYSICAL DAMAGE INSURANCE IS NOT INCLUDED)

NAME OF INSURANCE AGENT

ADDRESS OF INSURANCE AGENT

NAME OF INSURANCE COMPANY

CHECK COVERAGES

Comprehensive $ Deductible Collision Fire-theft and Combined Additional Coverage

SALESMAN

ORIGINAL

further confuse matters, the dollar amount of interest may be expressed as a percentage of the total amount you want to borrow and labeled the finance charge. Do not confuse a finance charge with interest. For example, say you want to borrow $100. You are told that the finance charge is 5%. Five percent of $100=$5,which is the *dollar* amount of interest you are paying on this loan. On the surface it may seem like your interest *rate* is also 5%. Not so. Remember, the interest is either added to or subtracted from the amount you want to borrow. Divide the number of payments by the total amount to figure your rate of interest. Let's say you are going to repay the $100 in one year (12 equal payments). If the interest is added to the loan value, figure 12 ÷105 =11.4% interest annually. If the interest is deducted in advance, figure 12 ÷ 95 = 12.6% interest annually. A good rule of thumb is to double the finance charge to obtain a rough idea of the annual interest rate.

Financing traps

Some dealers that advertise no down payment on their cars actually can make good on that claim, even if no trade-in is involved. The way they handle this is to finance a separate loan with a small lending company which covers the down payment. The interest on this loan is exhorbitantly high as a buyer who can't afford a down payment usually has a poor credit rating and may also be in personal financial difficulty—a bad credit risk. The buyer then faces the prospect of meeting payments on two separate loans. Missing payments on either one results in the car being repossessed.

The delayed payment ploy is another method of upping the interest rate in a finance agreement. Some states allow additional interest to be charged if the first payment on a loan is delayed 45 days or more. So while the buyer believes that he's getting a break by not having to come up with the initial payment for a while, he's getting socked with additional interest.

The balloon note is another unscrupulous practice for gouging the buyer. All the payments are for an equal amount except for the last one which is significantly higher. If you default on this last payment because you can't scrape together the additional money, you risk losing the car. Your alternative is to refinance the money due for this payment, netting the lender additional profits in the extra interest.

Some dealers get you on service fees. The car may be priced right and the financing arrangement may be in line. But service fees are just another way of adding to the finance charges, and your car isn't such a bargain after all.

You also might see a dealer advertising bank rates. What this means is that the dealer works closely with a particular bank and keeps sufficient funds on deposit to cover the dealer's endorsement of the buyer's installment contract. This protects the bank against loss and allows the dealer to enjoy a low interest rate. But this rate isn't necessarily enjoyed by you, the car buyer. You pay whatever agreement is negotiated between you and the dealer. The difference in rates that the dealer pays the bank and receives from the buyer is profit.

Quick Facts: Save Money On Financing

- Shop for lowest interest rates. Low interest sources: loans against savings account, life insurance and stocks; credit unions. Higher interest sources: banks; credit card plans. Highest interest sources: finance companies; car dealers.
- Always determine the annual rate of interest.
- Never finance a down payment.
- Make the largest down payment you can afford.
- Keep the number of payments to a minimum.
- Read the finance agreement carefully. Watch for service fees, large final payment and prepayment penalties.

Collision insurance can protect you from financial loss in case of a severe accident. If you finance, it'll be required.

More precautions

Check the financial agreement for prepayment penalties. If you think you might be able to pay off the loan before it is due, try to work out an arrangement with the lender for a reduction in the overall charges. Another clause sometimes written into the contract is a rebate at the end of the loan for paying on time. You'll probably have to fight for this one but it's the same money in your pocket as bargaining a few dollars off the car's price.

Buying insurance

When you buy a used car on time, the car dealer or lending institution requires that you carry certain insurance. This is a way of hedging their bet and reducing their chances of taking a loss. Remember, the car is still legally theirs until the last payment is made. To protect their car while you are tooling around in a hostile world, they require that you carry collision insurance. In case of a wreck, they know the car will be fixed and they won't find just a basket of parts on their doorstep. You'll be required to carry sufficient insurance to cover the value of the car.

If you buy a car privately, a good rule of thumb on collision insurance is to make sure that the premium you pay is no more than 15% of the car's current market value. You'll also save money on collision premiums if you take advantage of deductibles where you pay the first $100 or $250 of the repair bill.

You'll also be required to carry comprehensive insurance which covers you, though more so the dealer or lender, in the event of fire, theft, flood, windstorm or other catastrophes. These policies also have deductible features which can save you money on premiums.

Life/accident/health term policies may be insisted on by your creditor to guarantee their investment in case you die or become disabled and are unable to make

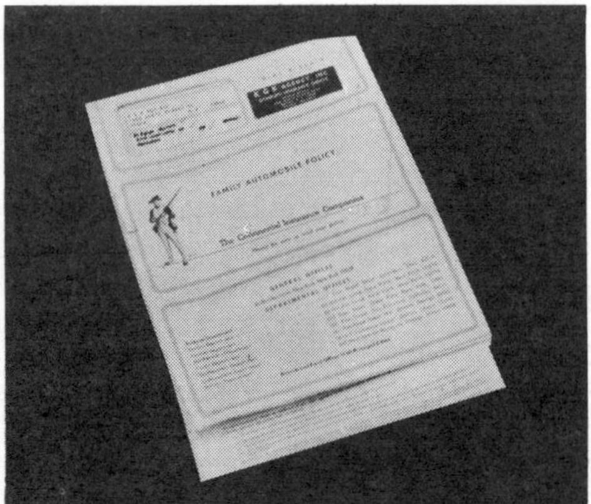

An automobile insurance policy can appear deceptively simple on the surface. . .

. . . .until you start to wade through it and realize it is a formidable document.

payments. You can save on this insurance if you already have your own coverage either privately or through your employment or union.

One little known type of insurance that is relatively inexpensive is called V.S.I. or Vendor's Single Interest. It insures payment of your outstanding debt to the dealer in case you total the car. You may find it difficult to obtain, but it's well worth the search because it can substitute for the much more expensive collision and comprehensive coverage.

Like car financing, insurance is available through different sources. The most convenient is through the car dealer, and like financing, it is also the most expensive. Car dealers love to sell you a complete package that includes insurance. What he does, in effect, is add the cost of insurance to the price of the car and then finance the total amount. So you're paying a very high interest rate on your insurance. You can save a heap if you shop for insurance in advance to get the best rates. Don't overlook obvious ways of saving money such as insuring with your regular company especially if they give discounts for a second car, or paying the premium in full to avoid finance charges entirely.

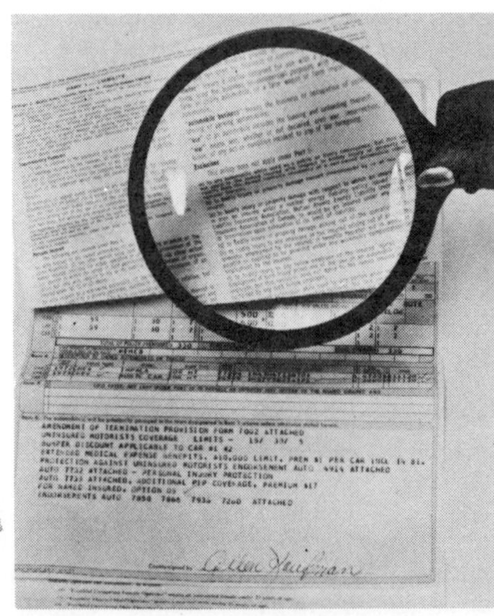

The fine print in your auto insurance policy spells out conditions of coverage.

Selling Your Present Car

A car maintained in good condition will bring a higher price when sold.

If you're reading this book, it's pretty safe to assume that you're in the market for a car, probably a previously owned car. It's also pretty safe to assume that you probably have a car now that you'll want to sell or trade on the new purchase.

Whether you're selling your present car privately or trading it to a dealer, you'll want to get every dollar you can out of it. Obviously, the better a car looks and runs, the better dollar value it will be to someone else and the more you'll be paid for it.

So your first job is to get your car into the best possible shape appearancewise. Your second job is to market your car effectively.

Preparing your car for sale

How much money your car will bring when sold, or how big an allowance when traded in, will depend a good deal on its condition. There are two ways to consider a car's condition: 1) apparent condition, 2) actual condition. If you intend trading your car in, it pays to concentrate on apparent condition. If you plan to sell privately, apparent condition is still the primary concern, but additional effort should go into your car's actual condition.

All car buyers, especially dealers, form a first impression by your car's overall appearance. A favorable first impression can go a long way in compensating for other shortcomings a car may have. Take a tip from the used car dealer. He details his cars so they present the best possible first impression. There's no reason why you shouldn't detail your own for the same effect.

In fixing up your car, spend no more than 15% of its retail value, and try to keep your expenses closer to 10%. If the car is worth $500 or less, limit your cash outlay to $50. Many items can be refurbished by elbow grease alone.

The primary concern, next to the car's ability to run, is the exterior and interior. A car wash is essential. Use either the garden hose variety or run through a commercial car wash. Applications of polish or rubbing compound will remove dead paint and restore some lost brilliance. Finish the job with a coat of wax for additional shine. You can do this the easy way by using a rotary buffer (electric drill). Don't forget to cover door jambs, panels under the hood and inside the trunk. Use chrome polish to remove rust and pits from chrome trim, bumpers, grille and wheel covers.

If you are selling privately, you should take care of some of the mechanical work. Change the oil and filter, and get a sticker

(continued on pg. 59)

Quick Facts: Stain Removal Guide

STAIN	VINYL	LEATHER	MOHAIR OR CLOTH
Blood	Use cold water before it sets. If dry, sponge with 1 tblspn. ammonia in 1 qt. water or scrub with strong detergent.	Same as for vinyl. If stain persists, feather lightly with damp Brillo.	Detergent in lukewarm water. Rub with nap. Do not use ammonia or bleach.
Catsup	Scrape off excess. Blot with water-soaked rag. Scrub stain with strong detergent.	Wipe away with damp sponge. If stain sets, use mild detergent.	Same procedure as for vinyl. Rub with nap.
Chewing Gum	Harden with ice cube, scrape off with dull knife. If pushed into fabric, use trichloroethane cleaning fluid.	Same.	Same.
Coffee	Blot with damp sponge. Then pour on plenty of warm water; blot up again with sponge. Trichloroethane removes cream stains.	Blot with damp sponge. Do not use water excessively, but scrub with powdered cleaners.	Same as for vinyl.
Crayon	Scrape with dull knife. Scrub with household cleaners on warm, damp sponge. If stain persists, use trichloroethane.	Same as for vinyl.	Same.
Ice Cream	Sponge with cold water. Rub detergent into spot or use trichloroethane fluid.	Same. May use cleanser, but sponge out excess.	Same as for vinyl.
Grass	Mix 1 quart alcohol with 2 parts water; sponge stain. Also try detergent rubbed hard into stain.	Same as for vinyl, but test small hidden area first to see if dye is colorfast to alcohol solution.	Same as for leather.
Grease and Oil	Scrub with trichloroethane first. To remove ring, rub with detergent or cleanser solution.	Same.	Same. Use plenty of water and mild detergent.
Ink (ballpoint)	Rub white petroleum jelly into stain, then rub with trichloroethane. Finally, sponge with strong detergent in warm water.	Do not use jelly. Rub with trichloroethane, then sponge with mild detergent or cleanser solution.	Same as for leather, but do not use cleanser.
Mildew	No problem with vinyl.	Let area dry, then scrape with dull knife. Sponge with soap or detergent.	Same as for leather.
Mustard	Rub glycerine into stain. Sponge off with detergent. If stain persists, rub with 1:2 solution of alcohol and water.	Let dry. Scrape excess with dull knife. Wash with 1:2 solution of alcohol and water, testing dye first.	Same as for leather.
Paint and Nail Polish	Before it dries, daub with rag dipped in turpentine or trichloroethane. Wash out rings with detergent. Never use paint thinner or nail-polish remover.	Test paint thinner or nail-polish remover on hidden area. If OK, daub painty area. If not, follow instructions for vinyl.	Same as for leather.

showing the mileage at which the job was done. If you've changed the oil regularly, leave the old stickers in place as proof of your attention to maintenance. If you've been haphazard about this type of service, remove all the old stickers.

A quick starting and smooth running engine is an important sales tool. A minor tuneup can pay for itself in a quick sale. Sometimes you can get away even less expensively by cleaning and adjusting the points, setting the dwell and timing and cleaning and regapping your old spark plugs. One trick that is sometimes used is advancing the ignition timing for more snap and using high test gasoline to avoid engine ping (except those cars which must operate on no-lead fuel).

Have the brakes adjusted if the pedal is low, and check the levels of all the fluids—engine oil, battery water, radiator coolant, auto transmission and power steering fluid, and brake fluid. Replace inexpensive items under the hood that appear obviously worn, like radiator hoses and use inexpensive temporary measures to correct defects like a leaking radiator or automatic transmission. Often, commercial chemicals for this purpose available in auto stores will fix things up—for a while, anyway.

When negotiating, if the potential buyer brings up defects you decided not to correct, tell him that you have taken them into account in your asking price.

Black tire paint is relatively inexpensive and available at auto accessory stores. Use it on all five tires, but be careful not to mark up whitewalls. You can clean whitewalls with steel wool soap pads. Clean the engine with a solvent that you can hose off with water. If your engine is extremely dirty, consider investing in a steam cleaning job, available at a nominal charge at some car washes.

Pay special attention to the trunk. Vacuum and wash it out. If the mat is very worn, it is not an expensive proposition to replace it. The interior should be thoroughly cleaned by vacuuming completely and shampooing the upholstery. Remove as many stains as you can from the seats

Glass can be replaced inexpensively at your local auto salvage yard.

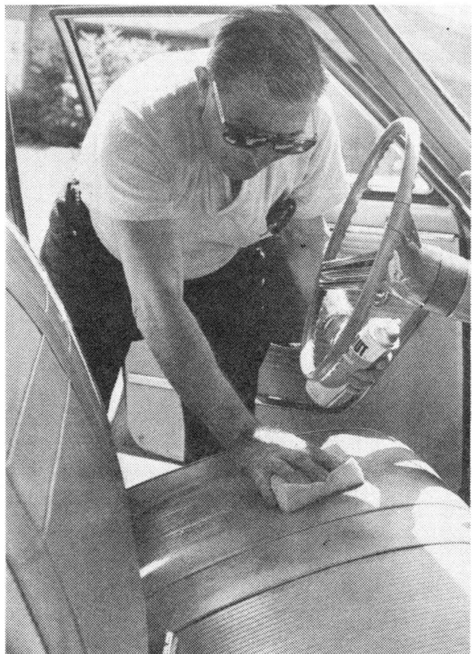

Shampooing upholstery is an easy job that can add dollars at resale time.

and the headliner. If the upholstery is badly worn or ripped, invest in a cheap set of seat covers.

You can buy replacement clutch, brake and accelerator pads at a discount auto store. But install them a couple of weeks in advance so they don't appear obviously new.

Cracked glass creates a poor impression, and it's not too expensive to replace if you shop your local junkyard. You usually can get the labor to replace the pane thrown in at little or no extra cost. Also use

Quick Facts: Preparing Your Car For Sale

- Wash, polish and wax the exterior.
- Remove all rust and pitting from bumpers, chrome trim and wheel covers with chrome polish.
- Replace broken glass, except damaged windshields and rear windows.
- Vacuum and wash out the trunk.
- Vacuum and shampoo the interior. Remove stains from the upholstery and headliner.
- Replace cracked lenses and small missing items like cigarette lighter, etc.
- Install inexpensive seat covers if upholstery is very worn or torn.
- Replace the trunk mat if it's very worn.
- (Stop here if you're trading to a dealer. Go on if selling privately.) Replace the accelerator, brake and clutch pedal pads.
- Adjust the brakes.
- Change the engine oil and filter and apply a new lubrication sticker.
- Remove the old lubrication stickers if you haven't been regular in your maintenance schedule.
- Minor engine tuneup if it's needed.
- Replace inexpensive obviously worn underhood items like radiator hoses.
- Clean the engine exterior.
- Top up all fluid levels—battery, engine oil, automatic transmission fluid, power steering fluid, brake fluid and radiator coolant.
- Install stop-leak chemical for cooling system leaks and automatic transmission sealer if necessary.
- Advance the engine timing and fill the gas tank with high test fuel (except those newer cars which must operate on no-lead fuel).
- Paint the tires.
- Clean the whitewalls.

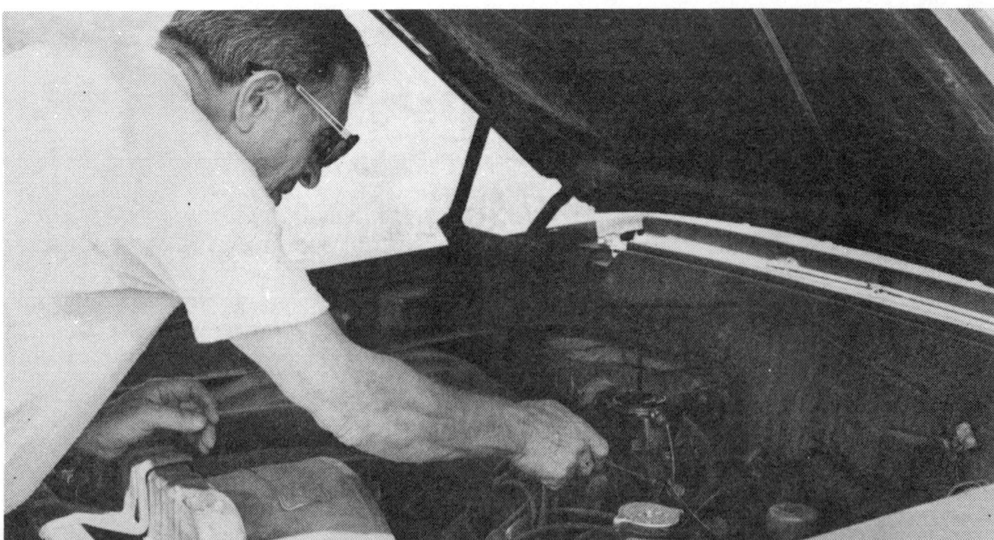

Simple engine tuning adjustments can be made by the seller himself at no expense.

the junkyard to replace items like cracked taillight and parking light lenses. Various and sundry items like cigarette lighters, mirrors and heat scarred ashtrays also are bargain priced at the junkyard. You can stop here if you plan to use the car for a trade. Any additional mechanical work can be done by the dealer cheaper than you can do it.

Creating an ad

The secret in selling your car through the classified section of your newspaper is to run an advertisement rather than just a listing. You'll notice that most private listings in the classifieds are the minimum three or four liners that cover just the bare bones and little else. That's because the minimum ad doesn't provide enough room for a selling job. Investing in more space to get your message across will sell a potential buyer rather than just inform him, and cause your ad to be more visible than the others.

Describe the car fully and include the color. Mention the condition of the exterior and interior separately. Your ad will have more impact if you use creative terminology rather than the stock descriptive phrases that appear in all the other ads. Something like "original upholstery has been maintained in new condition" tells the reader a lot more than the usual "like new" description covering the entire car.

The more details in your ad, the more interest it will generate. Mention specific drivetrain components especially if you have a desirable engine or gear ratio option. If you have a small V-8 engine, mention the cubic inch displacement and throw in a line about the outstanding fuel economy it delivers. Additions like "meticulously maintained" go far to create a feeling about your car in the reader's mind. And that's what Madison Avenue has been doing for years.

If you're the original owner, say so. It's a plus. List all the options on the car. Use standard abbreviations or spell them out for a really distinctive ad. Also, with certain exceptions, list any work that was recently performed. If you're selling a late model car, avoid mentioning any repairs that might arouse suspicion in the buyer. If you say the car has a rebuilt transmission, for example, the reader will wonder why a relatively new car had to have a new transmission. He might get the idea that the car was abused, or has subtantially more miles on it than you say in your ad. On a much older car, however, this can be a plus as major driveline components are more of a concern. If the engine and transmission on a new car are rebuilt, say "engine and transmission are in excellent condition," which would be true.

A clean trunk makes a favorable impression on a prospective buyer. Finish by vacuuming.

Don't forget to insert the word private before your phone number to eliminate suspicion that you may be a dealer.

Where to advertise

Use all the avenues of exposure that are mentioned in the chapter on "Where to Look." Use the same classified ad format on bulletin boards and other free spaces. If you choose to place a For Sale sign on your car, you can be briefer in your description as the car should be spruced up to sell itself.

Tips on selling

If you plan to sell privately, check the current market value of your car. You can do this by consulting used car price guide books, having your car appraised by several dealers or checking their prices on cars similar to yours.

You can find out the market value by visiting lending institutions and telling them you're interested in purchasing a car like the one you own. Check the local classifieds and find out the asking price of cars similar to yours.

Evaluating all these figures should give you a good idea of the spread between the current wholesale and retail price of your car. Set your price somewhere between the two depending on your car's actual condition. This is an honest way of approaching the situation. But each seller is governed by his own conscience. If your car is in above average condition, adjust your price closer to the retail market. But not too close, because a shrewd buyer will realize that for almost the same money as you are asking, he can buy from a dealer and work out a trade-in and obtain a guarantee.

Start off by quoting a price that will give you a margin to come down during negotiations. But don't make it so high that the buyer simply turns on his heel. During the bargaining, you can sweeten the pot by throwing in "extras" like spare parts and manuals that pertain to the car, or accessories like special dress-up mirrors and other options that you never got around to installing, or that you carefully removed specifically for this purpose. Be sure you didn't mention them in your advertisement.

Printed bills of sale can be obtained at most office supply and stationery stores.

If the buyer wants the car for a test ride or to have checked by his own mechanic, go along with him. More than one car has been stolen in this manner.

When a final agreement is reached, unless you know the person, insist on cash or a certified check for the full amount. If the buyer doesn't have the correct amount with him, tell him that you'll hold the car for x days for a modest deposit. Make your own decision as to whether the deposit will be refundable, and spell it out plainly on his receipt. Keep a copy of the receipt for yourself.

It's easy to get friendly during negotiations and many people of dubious honesty bank on this fact to throw a seller off guard. Remember, selling your car is a business transaction. Keep it on a strictly business level.

Quick Facts: Creating Your Ad

- Include the color of your car.
- Use creative phraseology but convey the message.
- Buy at least twice the minimum ad space.
- Mention specific engine and drivetrain components.
- If it's a small engine, mention outstanding fuel economy.
- Use phrases rather than single words to describe your car's condition.
- Describe separately the condition of the exterior, interior and mechanical components.
- If you're the original owner, say so.
- List all options and accessories.
- Insert the word private before your phone number.

Do-It-Yourself Repairs And Maintenance

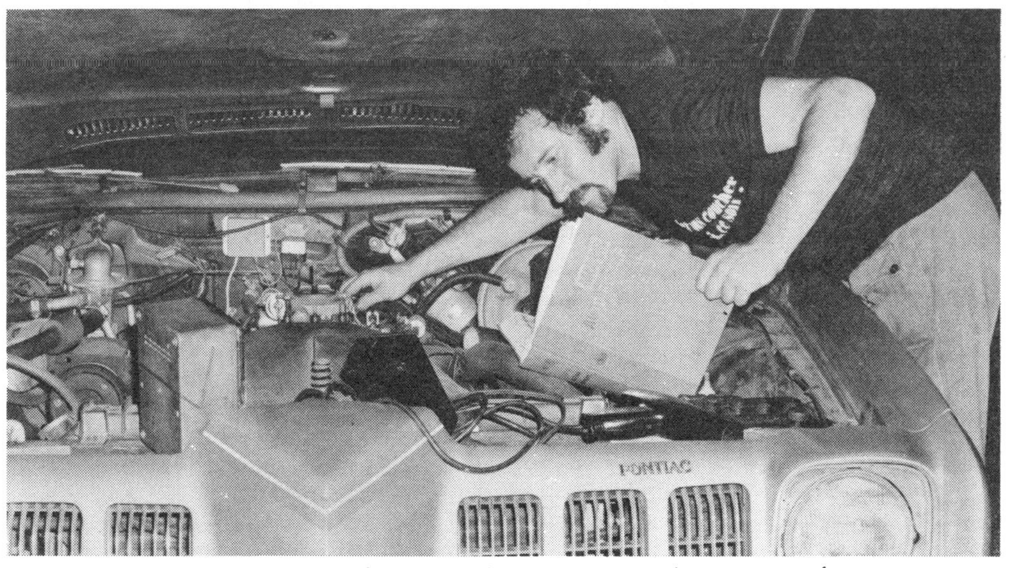

With a Motor repair manual as your guide, you can fix just about any part of any car.

One problem in owning any car, new or used, is its upkeep. Upkeep can be separated into two major categories—scheduled maintenance and unscheduled maintenance. The former consists of operations that the manufacturer suggests be performed at specified time or mileage intervals. These usually are spelled out in the owner's manual and include items such as oil change, filter replacement, lubrication and various inspections and adjustments involving everything from fan belts to the automatic transmission.

Unscheduled maintenance is more commonly referred to as repairs, and deals with fixing or replacing components that wear out or break. Examples of this type of service would include anything from boiling out a clogged radiator to replacing a rusted out exhaust pipe.

Keeping up with scheduled maintenance will increase a car's reliability and tend to cut down on repairs. The converse also is true.

Neglected air and oil filters will cause accelerated engine wear resulting in major damage and big repair bills. Allowing bad components to go unchecked can often lead to additional wear and damage of surrounding or related components, not to mention the possibility of creating an unsafe situation. Worn shock absorbers, for example, can shorten tire life and other suspension parts and cause loss of driver control in some situations. Radiator hoses that are in bad shape can cause engine overheating which in turn can cause serious engine damage.

If you expect your car to always start on demand and get you where you're going, it will need some help occasionally in the form of preventive maintenance.

Aside from preventing small repair jobs from developing into big ones, staying on top of your car's needs will pay dividends should you decide to trade or sell. The difference in what you'll receive could well run into hundreds of dollars. Documenting a car's history with service receipts will go much further than just appearance in convincing a prospective buyer of your car's worth.

The cost of car maintenance and repair

can vary widely. Severe usage like limited stop and go driving or hot rodding around town will accelerate wear and maintenance requirements. Another factor is where you have your car serviced. New car dealers are fine for work covered by warranty on either a new or used car. But their rates tend to be expensive when compared with other service outlets because of their high overhead costs. Independent repair shops and service stations are less expensive as long as you deal with one that's reputable.

More and more car owners are discovering that the real secret in saving on car maintenance is to do the job themselves. Many service operations are not as difficult as you might think. And if you're reading a book about used cars, you're probably dollar conscious anyway.

By far, the largest portion of your service dollar goes for labor. Eliminate the labor charge and reap substantial savings. Do-it-yourselfers are finding that their savings on service are not limited only to labor. Automotive parts, supplies and accessories are being offered at discount prices to do-it-yourselfers through mass merchandisers like Sears and Wards, automotive chain stores and regular wholesale parts houses that now also sell retail. And even your neighborhood supermarket may stock a line of automotive items.

Shade tree mechanics have assumed such sizeable proportions that whole industries have emerged to meet their automotive needs. Prepackaged tuneup kits containing all the components needed to tune the engines of most popular make cars, both imported and domestic, are available on a self-service basis through a variety of stores. Many non-automotive stores, like supermarkets, are stocking items such as motor oil and anti-freeze at substantially lower prices than you would pay at your local service station. The auto

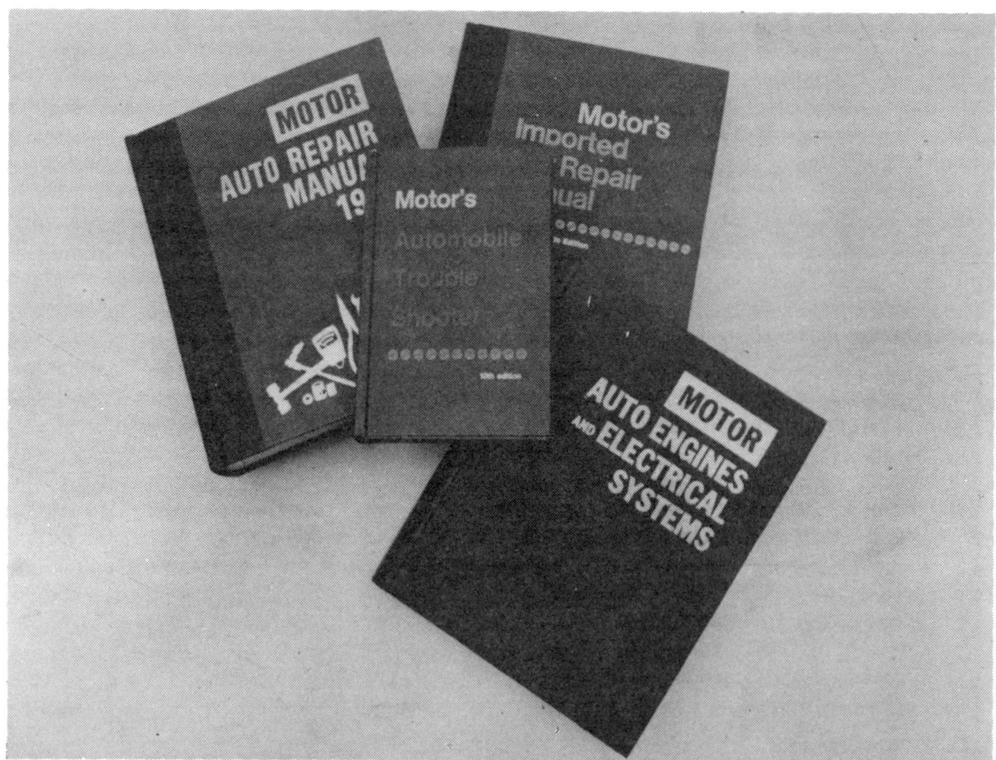

Motor's line includes the Auto Repair Manual for all domestic cars, a manual covering imports, the Trouble Shooter and Auto Engines book.

discount chains stock a complete line of the normal and specialized tools required for particular repairs along with complete selections of filters and other periodically replaced items, such as PCV valves, at moderate prices.

Special diagnostic equipment such as vacuum and compression gauges also are readily available to help the car owner troubleshoot engine problems and correct minor defects before they develop into major ones.

Many car owners offer the excuse of not doing their own maintenance and repairs by saying they don't know enough about what's under the hood. Or, if they have good mechanical ability, they're uncertain about the procedure for undertaking a particular repair.

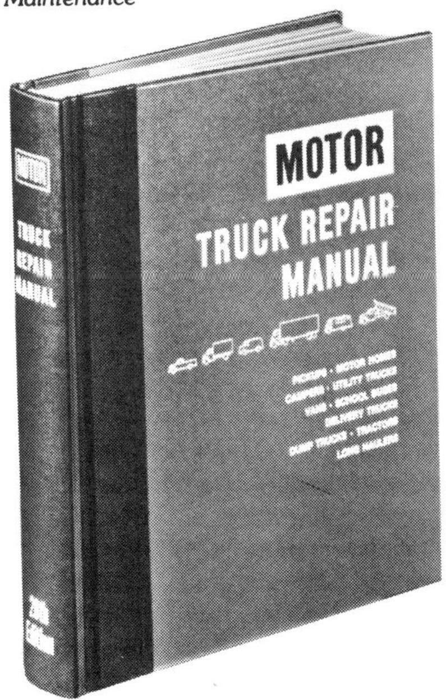

Motor's Truck Repair Manual covers pickups, vans, utility vehicles, etc.

That needn't be the case, especially today with the wide availability of repair guides such as Motor's series of repair manuals and troubleshooting guides. These are the same books used by thousands of professional mechanics. They take the reader step-by-step through just about all repair and troubleshooting procedures of any car. They feature special factory developed repair techniques and contain all the technical specifications needed for any job from torqueing down the cylinder head to the correct spark plug gap and engine idle speed.

The most widely used of these guides is the Motor Auto Repair Manual, referred to in the trade as the auto repairman's bible.

This is the same manual used in professional repair shops by mechanics who depend on it for correct repair procedures and specifications. The manual contains over 1000 pages with over 3000 detailed how-to pictures and diagrams covering all of the almost 3000 models of U.S. cars produced from 1969 through 1976. The manual also lists over 55,000 essential service specifications and adjustments. Through words and pictures it shows you how to fix carburetors, brakes, starters, engines, etc.

The most important part of auto repair is knowing what to fix. Like a medical doctor, you have to diagnose the problem from the symptoms before you can prescribe a cure. One of the most valuable features of Motor's Auto Repair Manual is its special section on troubleshooting with information that pinpoints scores of causes of car trouble. It gives you the reasons for slow or hard starting, engine knocks, pinging and stalling. It quickly spots where the trouble is in rear ends, clutches, steering systems and transmissions and then takes you step-by-step through the repair procedure. For a manual of this size and scope, it's very easy to use. The explanations and instructions are clear and concise and a special Instant Reference Index tells you the exact page to turn to.

For even more extensive troubleshooting information, check out Motor's Automobile Trouble Shooter. This is a glove compartment-sized guide that pinpoints over 2000 causes of car troubles. Designed for both the beginner and expert, the Trouble Shooter contains dozens of cutaway illustrations and diagrams that show important component parts in full detail. A special section on excessive fuel consumption points out conditions that greatly affect fuel economy. and the chapter on emergency highway procedures and trip planning are invaluable.

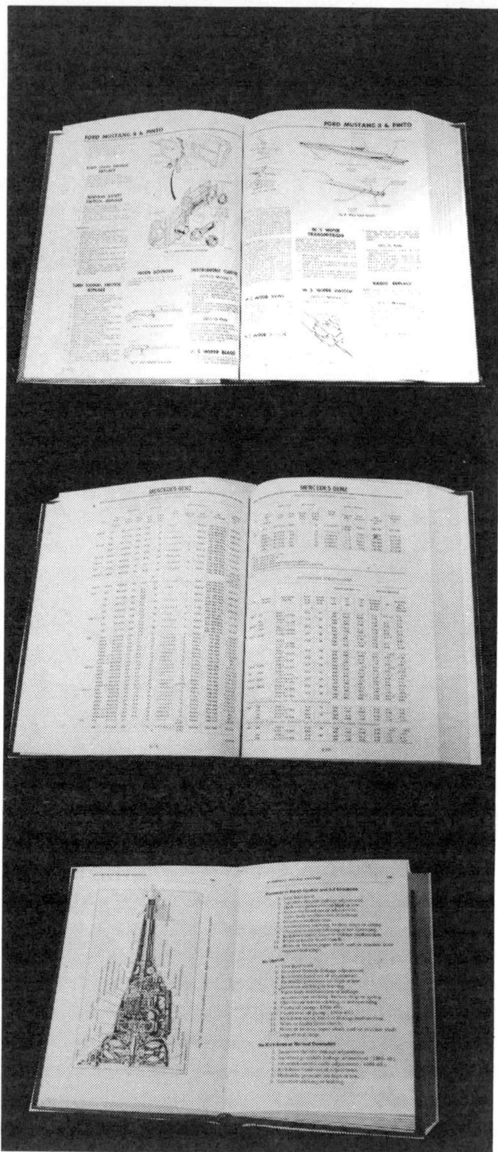

Top, the Auto Repair Manual is loaded with easy-to-follow instructions and diagrams. They give you enough information to fix almost any part of any car. Center, the Foreign Car Repair Manual gives you the same type of information for 25 makes of imports. Bottom, the Trouble Shooter pinpoints over 2000 car troubles.

If you own or are contemplating the purchase of an imported car, the Motor Foreign Car Repair Manual contains all the information needed to keep your car in cream puff condition. And like its domestic counterpart, this book features step-by-step maintenance procedures, thousands of specifications, hundreds of diagrams and illustrations and thousands of repair procedures for all popular imported car makes. Also included is a section on parts and tool availability that guides the imported car owner as to where he can buy the parts and special tools needed to keep his car in top running condition.

You'll find that the Motor Truck Repair Manual contains the same abundance of repair and tuneup information on pickups, vans, motor homes and other truck and utility vehicles.

For basic technical information and automotive design and repair theory, there's Motor's Auto Engines and Electrical Systems. This volume is used as a classroom textbook in thousands of automotive technology, auto shop and automotive engineering schools throughout the country.

While these guides aid the car owner in keeping his car in top running condition to provide economical and reliable transportation and top resale value, they also are an invaluable aid to the used car buyer. Not only can you more readily spot the symptoms of automotive problems, you can trace the trouble to its source and know exactly what's needed for repair.

You may know of car owners who decided to sell after their car developed a particular problem that the local mechanic diagnosed as an expensive proposition to repair. The car is bought by a mechanically knowledgeable person, is repaired for a modest sum and then resold at a handsome profit.

By far, the biggest bargain in used cars is the one that "needs mechanical work." Owners quite often overestimate a car's problem and run scared, letting it go for much less than it's worth. This is the perfect opportunity for the man who knows his cars. Using the Motor manuals and troubleshooting guides, he can diagnose the trouble and know what parts to replace. He can then accurately estimate the total cost of repairs and how much of a used car bargain he actually is getting. Quite often, Motor manuals have paid for themselves many times over on the first used car purchase or sale.